Cambridge Elements ≡

Elements in Metaphysics
edited by
Tuomas E. Tahko
University of Bristol

SUBSTANCE

Donnchadh O'Conaill
Université de Fribourg

Shaftesbury Road, Cambridge CB2 8EA, United Kingdom

One Liberty Plaza, 20th Floor, New York, NY 10006, USA

477 Williamstown Road, Port Melbourne, VIC 3207, Australia

314–321, 3rd Floor, Plot 3, Splendor Forum, Jasola District Centre,
New Delhi – 110025, India

103 Penang Road, #05–06/07, Visioncrest Commercial, Singapore 238467

Cambridge University Press is part of Cambridge University Press & Assessment,
a department of the University of Cambridge.

We share the University's mission to contribute to society through the pursuit of
education, learning and research at the highest international levels of excellence.

www.cambridge.org
Information on this title: www.cambridge.org/9781108940740

DOI: 10.1017/9781108935531

First published 2022

A catalogue record for this publication is available from the British Library.

ISBN 978-1-108-94074-0 Paperback
ISSN 2633-9862 (online)
ISSN 2633-9854 (print)

Substance

Elements in Metaphysics

DOI: 10.1017/9781108935531
First published online: October 2022

Donnchadh O'Conaill
Université de Fribourg

Author for correspondence: Donnchadh O'Conaill, doconaill@yahoo.co.uk

Abstract: Substance has long been one of the key categories in metaphysics. This Element focuses on contemporary work on substance, and in particular on contemporary substance ontologies, metaphysical systems in which substance is one of the fundamental categories and individual substances are among the basic building blocks of reality. The topics discussed include the different metaphysical roles that substances have been tasked with playing; different criteria of substancehood (accounts of what is it to be a substance); arguments for and against the existence of substances; and different accounts of which entities, if any, count as substances.

Keywords: substance, fundamentality, ontological categories, ontological dependence, grounding

ISBNs: 9781108940740 (PB), 9781108935531 (OC)
ISSNs: 2633-9862 (online), 2633-9854 (print)

Contents

1 Introduction

The notion of 'substance' has an illustrious and tangled history (see, e.g., Simons 1998; Robinson 2021). Rather than attempt to encompass this vast field, I have chosen to limit the scope of this Element in two respects. First, I shall be concerned primarily with substance as a specific *ontological category*. It is difficult to provide a brief informative gloss of ontological categories. A minimal characterisation is that they are general *kinds of entity*, 'the most general kinds under which things can be classified' (Loux 2006, 11). Other ontological categories, with which I shall contrast substances, include universal properties, tropes, events, and states of affairs.[1] In a *substance ontology*, the category of substance is one of the *fundamental categories*. That is, it is not the case that substances can ultimately be reduced to entities belonging to other categories (Loux 2006, 15; Lowe 2006, 58). The intuitive idea is that substances are among the fundamental entities, the 'basic building blocks' of reality. As we shall see, this idea can spelled out in a various ways.

It is worth briefly contrasting this notion of substance with two others. First, I shall set aside the notion of 'substance' as designating *stuffs* of various kinds (e.g., gold or water). On the notion of 'substance' as it is used in substance ontologies, substances are typically taken to be discrete particular entities rather than kinds of stuff. Second, the term 'substance' is sometimes used simply to designate any of a range of familiar concrete objects, such as trees, tables, or persons (Denby 2007, 473; Weir 2021, 268). This is not how I shall employ the term in what follows. This is not to say that none of these familiar objects count as substances. The point is that such entities count as substances in the sense that is relevant to this Element only insofar as they have certain characteristics or play certain theoretical roles. So while the term 'substance' as I shall use it may turn out to designate some or all of these entities, its meaning is different to the use of this term to mean any such entity. The use of the term 'substance' as meaning any such familiar concrete object is very close to what Kathrin Koslicki (2018, 164) terms the *taxonomic* use of the notion of substance, to pick out certain entities without committing oneself to their being metaphysically privileged. Koslicki contrasts this with a *non-taxonomic* use, on which the notion indicates that certain entities 'deserve to be assigned a special place relative to the ontology in question' (164). My use of the term 'substance' is non-taxonomic. Specifically, the special place substances occupy is that, if there are any, they are all fundamental or metaphysically basic entities (e.g., Loux

---

[1] On ontological categories, see Hoffman and Rosenkrantz 1994, 5–22; Westerhoff 2005; Lowe 2006.

1978, 165; Lowe 2006, 109; Robb 2009, 256; Heil 2012, 4; Jaworski 2016, 27; Inman 2018, 94).[2]

A corollary of this is that I shall by and large not engage with conceptions of familiar concrete objects as either bundles of properties or as combinations of properties and substrata (though see Section 6.1). I regard these conceptions as in effect claiming that familiar concrete objects are not substances as I intend to use this term (on these conceptions and on a conception of familiar concrete objects as substances in my preferred sense, see Loux 2006, 84–117).

The aim of this Element is to provide a systematic overview of substance as discussed in contemporary metaphysics (roughly, since the 1990s).[3] This indicates the second limitation on the scope of this Element. For the most part I shall not address the history of the notion of substance. Nor shall I consider contemporary work focusing primarily on historical exegesis (or if a work discusses both historical and contemporary themes I shall set aside those portions that focus on the former).

That said, it is worth briefly sketching some key points in the history of the notion of substance (for a more detailed overview, see Robinson 2021, section 2). One of the earliest appearances of this notion is in Aristotle's *Categories*. The opening pages of this work sketch an ontological system with four categories. Exactly how these should be understood is a matter of debate, but one common interpretation is as follows: first, accidental universals; second, essential universals (which Aristotle terms *secondary substances*); third, accidental particulars; and fourth, non-accidental particulars, which Aristotle calls *primary substances* (Studtmann 2021, section 1). An example of an accidental or non-substantial particular would be the whiteness of a particular sheet of paper, as opposed to the whiteness of any other sheet. An example of an accidental universal would be the universal property whiteness shared by all white objects. An example of an essential universal or secondary substance would be the universal human, under which each individual human falls. Examples of primary substances include individual humans and horses (Aristotle 1984a, 2a15). Primary substances are particular entities that bear or instantiate both essential and accidental universals and in which accidental particulars inhere; they are not themselves

---

[2] Note that it does not follow that all fundamental entities are substances.

[3] This is not to suggest that there had not been significant work on substance in prior decades (e.g., Anscombe 1964; Loux 1978; Wiggins 1980). But the 1990s saw the publication of three volumes (Hoffman & Rosenkrantz 1994, 1997; Lowe 1998), which together have led to a resurgence in discussions of substance in mainstream metaphysics. This has coincided with and contributed to a revival in neo-Aristotelian metaphysics (e.g., Schaffer 2009a; Tahko 2012; Novotný & Novák 2014).

instantiated by any other entities, and nor do they inhere in any other entities. In contrast, members of each of the other three categories are either instantiated by or inhere in other entities.

The notion of primary substance is a key source for subsequent work. That said, many later substance ontologies departed in various ways from the system just outlined. One of the first such departures was arguably undertaken by Aristotle himself in his *Metaphysics*. In this later work, Aristotle seems to conceive of the entities that in the *Categories* he had termed primary substances as being compounds of *matter* (very roughly, what each such entity is composed of) and *form* (the way matter is organised so as to make up each individual) (1984b, 1029a1–5). So, for instance, a particular bronze sphere is a compound of some matter (bronze) and a form (sphericity): 'we bring the form into this particular matter, and the result is a bronze sphere' (1033b9–10). This view is generally termed *hylomorphism*. On an influential reading, in Aristotle's hylomorphic system the genuine substances (or, at any rate, the most substantial or primary entities) are not entities such as an individual horse (a particular compound of matter and form) but forms, such as the form of the horse. The hylomorphic view of substance was extremely influential in medieval philosophy (see Pasnau 2011).

Substance was also a central category for the great early modern metaphysicians Descartes, Spinoza, and Leibniz. Broadly speaking, the early moderns did not develop accounts of substance by starting from paradigm examples (as Aristotle seems to do in the *Categories*).[4] Rather, each of them worked with a more abstract conception of substance as whatever is ontologically fundamental. Each of them cashed out the notion of fundamentality in slightly different ways, and each defended different views as to which entities count as substances. Very roughly, Descartes held that there are two distinct kinds of substance, extended and non-extended (substances whose nature consists in thinking). Spinoza and Leibniz each held that there is only one kind of substance, but while Spinoza famously argued that there is only a single entity of this kind (the cosmos, which he identified with God and which is both extended and thinking), Leibniz held that there are a plurality of non-extended thinking substances, the monads. For a brief overview of early modern views on substance, see Robinson's (n.d.) outline; for more detail, see Woolhouse's (1993) study.

---

[4] An exception to this might be God, which arguably each of these three rationalists regarded as a substance.

The present volume is structured around four questions about substance:

Q1 *roles*: which theoretical role or roles are substances posited to play?

Q2 *criteria*: what is it to be a substance?

Q3 *existence*: are there any substances?

Q4 *identification*: which entities, if any, are substances?

Adapted from Robb's (2009, 256) article, Q2–4 are more familiar from the recent literature than Q1. An answer to Q2 will at a minimum spell out informative necessary or sufficient conditions on an entity counting as a substance. More ambitiously, these conditions will tell us what it is for something to be a substance; they will explain why, for any given substance, it counts as a substance. An answer to Q3 will focus on arguments for thinking that there are (or must be) some substance or substances, or for thinking that there are (or must be) none. An answer to Q4 will consider entities we already take to exist, or which we at least think might exist, and ask which (if any) count as substances.

An answer to Q1 will specify the work which substances or the category of substance perform in different areas of philosophy. The role or roles played by substances provide the basis for arguments that there must be substances (i.e., answering Q3), and for attempts to identify which entities are substances (i.e., answering Q4). The different roles substances have been asked to play also suggest different criteria of substancehood (i.e., different answers to Q2). Therefore, the question of which roles substances might play, though less familiar than the other questions, is intimately related to them all.

I shall begin in Section 2 with a brief discussion of Q1. I shall then consider a number of different criteria of substancehood (Sections 3–5). In Sections 6 and 7, I shall consider Q3 and Q4, respectively.

2 Roles

2.1 Ontological Roles

The *role* of a category is the work that category is supposed to perform in a metaphysical system. (On different occasions I shall speak of categories or of their members as playing certain roles; I trust that the context will make clear what I mean.) One useful way to think of roles is in terms of solving problems that arise in metaphysical thinking (Oliver 1996, 11; Benovsky 2016, 66). The problem might be to *explain* a given phenomenon, and, as part of an explanation, certain entities are posited as bringing about the phenomenon in question. For instance, the truth of many propositions might be explained by positing states of affairs that make them true (Armstrong 1997, 116–19); or the similarities we observe between numerically distinct entities might be explained by positing universals that are shared by the similar entities (Loux 2006, 18). Other problems might involve *explicating* given phenomena, in the sense of saying more clearly what certain entities are. For instance, the problem might involve saying what, ontologically speaking, an ordinary concrete object is, and possible answers include a bundle of properties or a combination of properties and a substratum.

In each case, we can distinguish between the role that we posit entities to play and the entities that are posited (Oliver 1996, 11–12). For instance, states of affairs are often thought to play the truth-making role, but this role is not defined by reference to states of affairs, and other entities, such as tropes (Mulligan et al. 1984), have been proposed to play it. Jonathan Schaffer (2004, 93) puts the point nicely: for any entity of a given category, we can distinguish its *qualifications* for playing certain roles (those features of the entity in virtue of which it is apt to play a role) from the *responsibilities* it has insofar as it plays that role.

As Schaffer's formulation suggests, qualifications and responsibilities are closely linked. For instance, universals are often defined as being such that a single universal can be simultaneously instantiated by distinct entities. It is this characteristic of universals that makes them apt to account for similarities between distinct entities (e.g., Loux 1978, 3–10). The qualifications entities must have in order to play their assigned roles will be among the criteria for belonging to their ontological category.

The distinction between roles and the entities that fill them has been challenged by Jiri Benovsky. More specifically, Benovsky challenges the idea that we can offer any characterisation of an ontological posit that goes beyond stating its theoretical role.[5] The approach I take in this section is a version of what Benovsky (2016, 63) terms a *content view* of primitives, on which theoretical primitives have natures that are not exhausted by their playing certain roles. In contrast, Benovsky defends a *functional view* of theoretical primitives: 'primitives are individuated by what they do, what their functional role in a theory is, and, as a consequence, two primitives that do the same job just turn out to be equivalent for all theoretical purposes and metaphysically equivalent as well: they are just one and the same thing referred to in two different ways' (63). To claim that, in addition, primitives have non-functional content (and that different primitives have different non-functional contents) would be, Benovsky suggests, to postulate a difference that makes no difference to the theory itself (65).

---

[5] Benovsky (2016, 65 n. 1) limits his claim to *primitives*, non-analysable theoretical postulates introduced to perform specific tasks. He accepts that it may be possible that other entities have natures beyond the roles they play. Since the category of substance is plausibly a theoretical primitive, I shall restrict myself in what follows to what Benovsky says about primitives.

I shall raise two issues concerning Benovsky's defence of the functional view. To start with, we need to distinguish two different senses in which a theoretical primitive might be said to be *individuated*. The first way is to pick it out as a subject matter (i.e., in a way that fixes the reference of our terms). In this sense, a theoretical primitive certainly is individuated by its theoretical role, in that it is introduced precisely to play this role. But it does not follow that the nature of this entity (what it is, metaphysically speaking) is exhausted by its playing this role. So in a sense of 'individuate' that is more closely tied to saying what, metaphysically speaking, a specific entity is, a theoretical primitive might not be individuated by the role it is introduced to play. By way of comparison, a detective examining a crime scene might pick out a person by means of a definite description such as 'whoever made this footprint in the flower bed'. This description, if it is satisfied at all, individuates someone in this first sense of 'individuate'. But plainly it does not go very far to individuate anyone in the second sense. Benovsky seems to be mistaken in moving from primitives being individuated (in the first sense) by their theoretical roles to concluding that two primitives that play the same role are identical. At the very least, this argument can work only if supplemented by independent reasons to deny that theoretical primitives have any natures other than the theoretical roles they play.

A second issue with Benovsky's argument concerns what is involved in positing an entity to play a theoretical role. We can understand this procedure in terms of a certain *direction of fit*. The role is held fixed (i.e., the relevant problems are assumed to be genuine, and something is required such that by appeal to it these problems can be solved), and the posited entity is characterised so that it will fit this role. However, it does not follow from an entity's fitting a certain theoretical role that it thereby exists. The majority of contemporary metaphysicians are *ontological realists*, accepting that 'there are facts of the matter about ontology, which are objective' in the sense of obtaining regardless of our activities or interests (Jenkins 2010, 881). That is, one can formulate a conception of entities of a certain category, the Cs, and one can posit Cs to play a certain role, but this does not determine whether or not there are any Cs. What determines this is whether or not one's description of the Cs succeeds in picking out entities that match this characterisation.[6] So when we move beyond positing entities as playing a theoretical role to consider whether or not they exist, the direction of fit is different: the posited entity exists only if its characterisation

---

[6] This is a simplification. In many cases, it may be possible to adjust one's conception of Cs while still positing them as entities of the same category. But there are limits to how far one can do this: at some point, one will in effect have changed the subject, moving from positing Cs to positing entities of a different category, Ds.

fits with something in the world, and it is this worldly entity that is fixed in the sense that (at least typically) it exists regardless of how (or whether) we chose to think about it.

This view of ontology is not mandatory. There are ontological anti-realists, and Benovsky (2016, 124–5) himself has sympathies with such a view: he suggests that metaphysical theories are not true or false, and that metaphysics does not consist in statements about how the world is. But the vast majority (perhaps all) of the philosophers who posit substances are ontological realists. That is, they regard statements to the effect that there are substances, or that such-and-such entities are substances, as truth-apt, and they regard them as true (or false) regardless of our activities or interests (unlike, for instance, the truth of statements about fashion trends or monetary policy).

I cannot address the general dispute between ontological realists and anti-realists in this Element. But insofar as there is reason to accept ontological realism (or at least no convincing reasons to reject it), one is entitled to distinguish the roles substances might play from their other characteristics, and in particular from different criteria of substancehood.

2.2 Roles Played by Substances

Let us now consider which roles the category of substance might be tasked with playing. One approach to this issue starts with a conception of reality as stratified into levels of entities that are more or less metaphysically fundamental. This conception is not strictly pre-theoretical, but nor is it wedded to any specific theory (compare with Koslicki 2018, 138–9). Rather, it takes different forms in different theoretical contexts. One manifestation was the medieval idea of the Great Chain of Being, on which God was the most metaphysically important entity, followed by angels, humans, organisms, and non-organic entities (Lovejoy 1964). (In the Great Chain of Being, God was often placed at the top of the hierarchy, whereas in other versions of the hierarchical picture the most metaphysically important entities are at the bottom. In what follows, I shall generally speak of the most important entities as being at the bottom of the hierarchy.) More recently, reality has been understood as structured in a way corresponding to a reductionist hierarchy within the sciences, on which in principle each science could be reduced to that beneath it, with physics (specifically micro-physics) at the bottom.

Hierarchical conceptions of reality give rise to various problems, one of which is the question of whether the hierarchy of levels goes down forever. This problem can be addressed in various ways (see Section 6.1). But those who wish to retain the hierarchical view and who cannot accept unending descent must posit a lowest level, an entity or entities such that there is nothing more fundamental. This is a role, that of being the *foundation of being*, that substance is traditionally thought to play:

> [T]he substances, in addition to being themselves ontologically independent, must also act as a sort of 'ontological anchor' for all the other entities that are included in the ontology under consideration … everything which does *not* qualify as a substance (i.e., every entity, *y*, that is not ontologically independent and hence ontologically depends on some relevant, *z*, numerically distinct from *y*) ontologically depends on something which *does* qualify as a substance (i.e., on something that is ontologically independent).[7] (Koslicki 2018, 168 n. 8)

This role is closely linked to a conception of substances as ontologically independent (see Section 3). Specifically, if one assumes a hierarchical conception of reality with a lowest level, then not only will one want to posit entities on which all else depends; one will also want these entities to not themselves depend (or at least not depend in the same way) on anything else. (If these entities were themselves dependent on other entities, then they would not together form the *lowest* level in the hierarchy, and indeed the structure would be more holistic or circular than hierarchical.)

That said, it is important to note that this role of foundation of being is not the same as the characteristic of being independent. To see this difference more clearly, consider a view of reality on which there are no hierarchies of ontological dependence: no entity depends, in any of the ways to be considered in the next section, on any other. In this 'flatworld' every entity would be ontologically independent, but no entity would play the theoretical role of standing at the bottom of the hierarchy of being.

As is the case with the other roles mentioned, there are multiple candidates to play this role. It has been held that the fundamental entities are universal properties, with other entities being constructed out of them (O'Leary-Hawthorne & Cover 1998). Or the fundamental entities might be tropes, particular properties out of which all other entities are constructed (Campbell 1990). Neither of these views is compatible with a substance ontology, given that substances cannot be identified with either universal properties or with tropes (see Section 6.3). That said, a substance ontology is compatible with there being other fundamental entities in addition to substances.

The role of foundation of being is arguably the most central role that the category of substance has been asked to play. However, substances have also

---

[7] Note that Koslicki does not accept that substances play this role, or that they are ontologically independent. This role of foundation of being is arguably distinct from, though closely related to, the role of explaining why the other entities in the hierarchy exist (Robb 2009, 258). This other role suggests a grounding or explanatory criterion of substancehood (Section 4).

been pressed into service in response to other problems. As an example, consider a more localised metaphysical question: the nature of selves. By 'self' I simply mean a subject of experiences, an entity that has or can have conscious experiences.

In considering the nature of selves, we are faced with certain widely accepted pre-theoretical assumptions. For instance, it seems that anything that is a self will be capable of persisting through changes in its experiences (i.e., of having a painful experience at time $t1$ and different experiences, none of which are painful, at $t2$). Likewise, it should be possible for a self to not have had at least some of the experiences it actually has had; and it should be possible for a self to have had experiences other than those it actually had. For instance, suppose you had chosen a radically different course of work or study; in that case, you would very probably not be having the experiences you are currently having while reading these words, but would rather be having different experiences.

These assumptions can be understood as together carving out a theoretical role, that of categorising selves in such a way that they have these characteristics. And one way to categorise selves such that they have these characteristics is by classifying them as substances. As E. J. Lowe (1996, 195) put it, the self has 'the status of a substance vis-à-vis its thoughts and experiences – they are "adjectival" upon it (are "modes" of it, in an earlier terminology), rather than it being related to them rather as a set is to its members'. This way of thinking of selves and their experiences is closely linked to the Ultimate Subject criterion of substancehood (see Section 5.1).[8] When one thinks of selves in this way, it is clear that the very same self could have existed without having the experiences it actually had, and that it can persist through changes in its experiences. That is, selves understood as substances can fill the role carved out by the assumptions outlined in the previous paragraph (see also Section 7.4).

Again, substances are not the only ontological category that can fill this role. For instance, bundles of capacities to produce experiences (Dainton 2008) could arguably do so as well. But in the present context all that is being claimed is that there is a distinctive role here, and that understanding selves as substances is one way to fill it.

In principle, a similar role can apply to other entities. It is commonplace to think that there are many other entities (e.g., organisms, planets, molecules) that can persist through changes in their intrinsic properties, that could have failed to have some of the properties they actually had, and that could have had properties other than those they actually had. So we can generalise the role just

---

[8] The notion of 'subject' in the Ultimate Subject criterion is not restricted to subjects of experience; roughly speaking, it picks out anything that can bear properties. Entities that are not subjects of experience can be subjects, indeed ultimate subjects, in this broader sense.

described to apply to any such entities. And for any such entities, thinking of them as substances is one way to fulfil this role (i.e., of understanding them as able to persist through changes, etc.; e.g., Hoffman & Rosenkrantz 1994, 23; Simons 1998, 237–8).

So there are at least two distinct roles that substances have traditionally been tasked with playing. These roles do not obviously fit together; for instance, it is not obvious that selves as just described belong to the foundations of being. One response to this would be to conclude that there are distinct conceptions of 'substance', each earmarked to play one of these two roles. Indeed, one could go further. Perhaps there are distinct categories, each of which is confusingly labelled 'substance'. And it might be that the different criteria for substancehood outlined in the next three sections are in fact criteria for distinct categories of entity. A similar issue has cropped up in debates about properties: different property roles have been proposed and it has been suggested that there are different categories of entity that play different roles. For instance, David Lewis (1983) explores the idea that universals play some of the property roles and classes of possibilia play others.

But it might also be thought that the two roles complement each other and together indicate a richer notion of substance. Recall that in Section 1 I said I would focus on the notion of substance as used in substance ontologies. At least in many such ontologies, substances have been deployed to play both the roles I have outlined (see, e.g., Loux 2006, 108; Lowe 2006, 109; Schaffer 2009a, 378–9).

Combining the roles in this way also allows for a response to an issue raised by Koslicki. She points out that a number of philosophers (e.g., Lowe 1998, 159; Schnieder 2006, 396; Heil 2012, 93; Wiggins 2016, 1) stipulate that substances are particulars, but argues that this begs the question against those philosophers who maintain that the most fundamental entities are universals (Koslicki 2018, 138–9). In one sense, Koslicki is correct. If substances are understood simply as whichever entities are fundamental (e.g., as whatever plays the role of foundation of being), then it is question-begging to assume at the outset that they must be particulars. But many proponents of substance ontologies work with a richer notion of substance. On this richer notion, there are principled reasons to exclude universals from the category (for instance, universals seem ill-fitted to play the second role for substances outlined earlier). Nor does this beg the question against those who claim that the fundamental entities are universals. Rather, what we have here are two rival conceptions of the fundamental entities; as including substances understood as particulars, or as limited to universals (see also Robinson 2021, introduction).

Each of the roles I have outlined prompts the question of what substances must be like in order to be able to play it. This question takes us directly to possible *criteria of substancehood*, which will be discussed in the next three sections.

3 Criteria of Substancehood: Independence

3.1 Methodological Preliminaries

Before discussing different criteria it is worth mentioning some methodological distinctions. The first concerns whether or not one assumes specific examples of substances. If one does, then whether or not a proposed criterion fits these examples will in effect serve as a standard against which it can be measured. Such paradigmatic substances often include 'ordinary' objects like organisms, artefacts, or planets (e.g., Ayers 1991, 69; Hoffman & Rosenkrantz 1997, 1; Lowe 1998, 164; Simons 1998, 239; Correia 2005, 128; Gorman 2006, 116; Schnieder 2006, 393–4; Oderberg 2007, 66). They may also include more recherché entities such as God or immaterial souls. Correlatively, Fabrice Correia (2005, 128) offers a list of what he regards as paradigmatic *non-substances*: 'events, states, tropes, universal properties and relations, sets, holes and surfaces'. These might be thought to provide a further standard, in that a proposed criterion that encompasses such entities is thereby not satisfactory.

In contrast, one might assume few if any paradigmatic examples of substances. Proponents of this approach tend to stress that substances must be apt to play certain theoretical roles or meet very demanding criteria; consequently, they tend to be more revisionary regarding our pre-theoretical beliefs about which entities count as substances. On this approach, examples such as those just listed may provide a sense of what it is for something to be a substance (e.g., as opposed to a property), but on further consideration we may realise that they are not themselves substances, strictly speaking (Heil 2012, 4, 20).

These approaches need not be diametrically opposed; it may be more accurate to say that in constructing and evaluating accounts of substancehood different philosophers will emphasise each to different degrees. Nevertheless, the difference between these approaches becomes evident when we consider the lists of substances that different philosophers have drawn up (see Section 7).

A second methodological distinction concerns what one is trying to do in proposing a criterion. One approach stresses *methodological neutrality*: we should aim 'to provide a characterization of substance which is, as far as possible, neutral with respect to particular metaphysical positions' (Correia 2005, 128). For instance, we should try to formulate a criterion of substance that does not presuppose a particular ontology, such as whether or not entities of a certain kind exist (Hoffman & Rosenkrantz 1997, 13). The advantage of a methodologically neutral criterion is that it can be applied to a wide variety of positions, allowing us to contrast different ontological frameworks using categories common to each.

But one might propose a criterion of substancehood that is more closely tailored to a specific philosophical view. This view might concern one's prior assumptions as to which entities count as substances, or it might involve a relatively austere ontology (i.e., one might want to strictly limit which kinds of entities one posits). The general point is that one may already be committed to a philosophical view and may want to use the notion of substance to elucidate it better (e.g., Lowe 2013, 203).

A final preliminary point is that, as mentioned in Section 1, a proposed criterion of substancehood can be understood in different ways: as stating an (informative) *necessary condition* on an entity's being a substance, as stating a *sufficient condition*, or as providing an account (either complete or in part) of *what it is* for an entity to be a substance. In what follows, I shall occasionally refer to these different ways of understanding proposed criteria, but for the most part I shall remain neutral between them.

3.2 Approaching the Criterion of Independence

Perhaps the most popular criterion of substancehood is Independence: substances are independent entities. This criterion can be developed in a number of ways, which can usefully be distinguished by answers to two further questions:

(a) What kind of independence? That is, in what way are substances independent entities?

(b) Independent from what? That is, what are the entities from which substances are independent? (Crane 2003, 239; Denby 2007, 473–4)

There are various ways in which entities can be dependent. For instance, one event can *causally depend* on others, and certain concepts *conceptually depend* on others (e.g., the concept 'bachelor' depends on the concept 'marriage'). In what follows, I shall set aside these forms of dependence, and formulate different answers to (a) in terms of different versions of *ontological dependence*. In discussing these, I shall also consider various options regarding (b).

3.3 Existential Independence

To start with, we can say that an entity is *existentially dependent* if it cannot exist unless some other entity or entities exist. More specifically, we can distinguish between rigid and generic existential dependence (Correia 2008, 1014–16; Tahko & Lowe 2020, section 2):

An entity x is *rigidly existential dependent* on an entity $y =_{\text{def}}$ necessarily, if x exists then y exists.

An entity x is *generically existential dependent* on some F or $Fs =_{\text{def}}$ necessarily, if x exists then some F exists.[9]

In the case of rigid dependence, x cannot exist unless y (that very entity) also exists. Consider a collection or sum of entities, such as a particular bell, book, and candle. This collection cannot exist unless these very entities do; it is the collection of these very entities, not of any others. In contrast, if x generically depends on an F, it does not need any specific F in order to exist; some other F would do just as well. For instance, it is plausible that a cat cannot exist unless composed of cells of a certain type, but plausibly it need not be composed of any specific cells of that type.

From these notions of existential dependence, we can straightforwardly define correlative notions of independence. An entity x is *rigidly existentially independent* if it is not the case that, necessarily, if x exists then some particular entity y exists. This leaves open the possibility that x cannot exist unless some other entities also exist, even if there is no specific other entity that must accompany x. *Generic existential independence* captures the idea that x can exist unaccompanied by any entity of a specific type. And if F is taken to range over any entity whatsoever (other than x itself), it can be used to capture the idea that x can exist unaccompanied by any other entity.

These notions of ontological independence suggest two distinct criteria of substancehood (Lowe 1998, 138, 141):

> Rigid Existential Independence Criterion (REIC): An entity x is a substance $=_{\text{def}}$ necessarily, there is no entity y such that x rigidly existentially depends on y.

> Generic Existential Independence Criterion (GEIC): An entity x is a substance $=_{\text{def}}$ necessarily, there are no entities of type F such that x generically existentially depends on any entity or entities of type F.

For example, consider Descartes' (1985, 1:51) characterisation: 'By substance we can understand nothing other than a thing which exists in such a way as to depend on no other thing for its existence.' This can be understood as an expression of either REIC or GEIC, depending on how we understand the phrase 'no other thing' (for differing interpretations of Descartes on this score, see Hoffman & Rosenkrantz 1997, 21; Correia 2008, 1025; Weir 2021, 284–7).[10]

---

[9] I shall use 'necessarily' and other modal notions to express *metaphysical modality*. In formulating different kinds of dependence, I assume that x is not numerically identical with y or with any of the Fs. I shall use the letters 'x', 'y', and so on for ease of presentation. These are standardly used as variables, but in certain places (as in the definition of rigid existential dependence), I shall use them to denote specific entities; I trust that the context will make clear how they are being used.

[10] An added complication is that Descartes (1985, 1:51) thought that each created entity depended for its existence on God, so strictly speaking God was the only substance. However, Descartes

There are numerous counter-examples to REIC and GEIC (see Lowe 1998, 138–47; Schnieder 2006, 399–400; Correia 2008, 1025–6; Inman 2018, 64–6; Koslicki 2018, 142–4). First, given certain background assumptions they threaten to rule out all (or virtually all) candidate substances. Consider the possibility that there are necessarily existing entities (e.g., God, or mathematical objects if Platonism about mathematics is correct). If y is a necessarily existing entity, then trivially no other entity can exist unless y exists. Therefore, no entity (perhaps other than y) could satisfy either REIC or GEIC. Furthermore, it may be that for every entity x there is some distinct entity y which necessarily co-exists with it (i.e., it may be that necessarily, x exists iff y does). For instance, on certain assumptions every entity is the sole member of a specific set (its singleton). It is often thought that each set exists iff its members exist. Given these two assumptions, it is necessarily true that each entity is accompanied by its singleton. Each entity would be rigidly (and generically) existentially dependent, and so no entity could be a substance.

Second, these criteria give rise to further problems for specific kinds of candidate substance. For instance, REIC rules out any candidate substance that necessarily has specific entities as proper parts. Suppose that a particular water molecule necessarily has a specific oxygen atom as one of its proper parts; given REIC, it would follow that this water molecule could not be a substance (Gorman 2006, 114). Given GEIC, any candidate substance that necessarily has entities of a certain kind among its proper parts would be ruled out (even if it does not necessarily have any specific entity of that kind as a part).

Likewise, REIC rules out any candidate that necessarily has a specific property, or necessarily undergoes a certain event. If GEIC applies, any candidates that necessarily have properties of a certain kind or necessarily undergo events of a certain kind will be excluded. If REIC applies, it will rule out any entity that necessarily originates from, say, specific distinct entities (e.g., a specific sperm and egg). Finally, GEIC seems to rule out any entity that necessarily originates from entities of a certain kind.

There are various strategies available in response to this battery of problems. One option is to bite the bullet, for instance by accepting that there are no substances, or no complex substances. At this stage of inquiry such responses seem premature. Apart from anything else, they overlook the possibility that there are other ways of framing Independence, and indeed that there are other criteria of substancehood to consider.

---

suggested that we could consider other entities as substances if we set this dependence on God aside. This is an example of an answer to question (b) mentioned earlier.

Another strategy is to reject the assumptions required to generate the counter-examples. For instance, one might deny that there are any necessarily existing entities, or deny that every entity is such that necessarily some other entity co-exists with it (e.g., one might deny that there are sets). While the resulting combination of views may be coherent, there is always the danger that it is ad hoc; that one is adjusting one's other views in order to save one's preferred conception of substance. This strategy also violates the principle of methodological neutrality mentioned in Section 3.1.

A third strategy is to work around some of the counter-examples by limiting the scope of the criteria in various ways. This brings us to (b) mentioned in Section 3.2. Up until now, we have understood 'y' in REIC and 'some F' in GEIC as ranging over any entities whatsoever (except for x itself). But it might be thought that this requirement is too stringent; intuitively, there are certain entities that x can depend upon while still counting as a substance, as a basic building block of reality. That is, we would adjust REIC or GEIC by restricting the scope of the entities from which a substance must be independent. One way to do this is to set aside dependence on necessarily existing entities. The thought here might be that such dependence is a trivial product of these entities existing necessarily; since it applies equally to every entity whatsoever, we can in effect 'cancel through' all necessarily existing entities when it comes to evaluating existential independence.

Another way to develop this thought is as follows: what we require of a substance is that it not depend on anything *external* to it for its existence. This is compatible with its depending on what is *internal* to it (Weir 2021, 295–7). The relevant notions of 'internal' and 'external' can be understood in different ways. For instance, one might think that an entity contains all of its proper parts, if it has any. So REIC could be adjusted as follows:

> REIC*: An entity x is a substance $=_{\text{def}}$ necessarily, there is no entity y such that (A) y is not a proper part of x, and (B) x rigidly existentially depends on y.
> (compare with Fine 1995, 269–70; Simons 1998, 236)

Or one might consider x's *intrinsic properties* (roughly, the properties x has in and of itself, regardless of what else exists) to be internal to it.[11]

The final option available is to give up REIC and GEIC. One might think that the root cause of the problems we have been discussing lies in the conception of ontological dependence as existential dependence. This is not to say that ontological dependence has nothing to do with existence. But existential dependence seems too coarse-grained to capture the sense in which substances

---

[11] For discussion of these kinds of adjustments, see Toner 2011; Gorman 2012; Koslicki 2018, 179–84.

do *not* depend on other entities. In response to this kind of worry, theorists have proposed a number of different conceptions of ontological dependence.

3.4 Essential Independence

One well-known alternative to existential dependence is essential dependence. This conception of dependence involves a *non-modal* conception of essence. To introduce this, let us first consider what a *modal* conception of essence involves. Roughly, we can say that certain *de re* truths about an entity, x (hereafter 'truths about x'), are necessarily true of x: they are true of x in any possible circumstance where x exists. In contrast, other truths about x are only contingently true of x; they could be false even in circumstances where x exists. A modal conception of essence regards all necessary truths about x as essential to it, and regards these truths as together stating or expressing what is essential about x.

On a non-modal conception of essence, it is not the case that *all* necessary truths about x are essential to x (though it is usually assumed that all essential truths about x are necessarily true of x). One familiar example is Socrates's being the sole member of his singleton set, {Socrates}. Given standard assumptions, it is necessarily true of Socrates that he belongs to {Socrates}. However, there is a sense of 'essential' on which this is not essentially true of Socrates; it is not part of Socrates's essential nature, of what he fundamentally is, that he is a member of this or any set.[12]

The non-modal conception of essence yields a correlative notion of essential dependence:

> x is *essentially dependent* on $y \equiv_{\mathrm{def}} y$ is a constituent of x's essence. (Koslicki 2018, 154)

We can say that y is a constituent of x's essence if y is mentioned in an essential truth about x (Fine 1995, 275). For instance, it is essentially true of {Socrates} that it has Socrates as its member; therefore, {Socrates} essentially depends on Socrates. In contrast, plausibly there is no essential truth about Socrates that mentions {Socrates}; therefore, Socrates does not essentially depend on {Socrates}. This is so even though it is necessarily true of Socrates that he is a member of {Socrates}. In this way we can see how essential dependence is more fine-grained than existential dependence.

---

[12] Kit Fine, whose example this is, develops his non-modal conception of essence by appeal to an entity's *real definition*, a statement of what that entity is (as opposed to a nominal definition, a statement of the meaning of a word). On real definitions, see Koslicki 2012; Correia 2017. My sketch of the non-modal conception of essence omits certain details, such as the distinction between constitutive and consequential essence (Fine 1995, 276–9; Koslicki 2018, 154–8).

I have formulated essential dependence in terms of rigid dependence, but an entity can also generically essentially depend on entities of a certain type. Consider again the example of a cat and its cells. It is plausibly essential to each cat that it must be composed of cells of a certain type, but a cat does not seem to be essentially composed of any specific cells of this type.[13]

The notion of essential dependence can be used to formulate a version of Independence:

> Essential Independence Criterion (EIC): An entity x is a substance $=_{\text{def}}$ necessarily, there is no entity y such that x essentially depends on y.

A view like EIC is discussed by Fine (1995, 287). His discussion contains additional subtleties, which I shall not be able to address.

At least some of the counter-examples facing REIC and GEIC are avoided with EIC. It is compatible with substances that necessarily are members of sets, and with necessarily existing entities. It is also compatible with substances necessarily having properties or parts that are not essential to them; for example, I necessarily have the property *being either alive or not alive*, but plausibly this is not part of what I essentially am.

However, it is not clear if EIC avoids all of these counter-examples. For instance, it seems possible for substances to essentially have certain properties (e.g., it may be essential to me that I exist in time). At least some complex entities seem to have certain parts essentially (e.g., a molecule and its atoms). And while a cat might not essentially have any specific cell as a part, it might be essentially composed of *some* cells of a specific kind. In this case, EIC would seem to rule out such organisms as substances.

Koslicki outlines two further counter-examples to EIC, of which I shall consider one (the other being the empty set; see Koslicki 2018, 160). We can understand natural numbers other than 0 as constructed from 0 via applications of the successor relation (1 is the successor of 0, 2 is the successor of 1, and so on). Therefore, there will be an essential truth about each natural number that mentions some other natural number (the number of which it is a successor). But 0 is not constructed in this way. Indeed, its essence seems to be 'simple and non-relational, in the sense that what it is to be that very number is not defined in terms of its relation to any other natural number' (Koslicki 2018, 161). So EIC seems to commit us to a peculiar ontological division within the natural numbers, into those that are not substances and the number 0, which is.

---

[13] For discussions and formulations of generic essential dependence, see Fine 1995, 287–9; Correia 2008, 1017; Lowe 2013, 194; Inman 2018, 68.

It is true that for many classes of entities we would not expect different members of the same class to belong to different ontological categories. But given how Koslicki characterises natural numbers, this class of entities is different to most other classes. It is a class where all members except one are constructed from that member of the class (i.e., 0).[14] In other words, on this characterisation there is an ontological asymmetry between 0 and all other natural numbers. Given this, it does not seem so unreasonable to think that 0 might be a different kind of entity, ontologically speaking, than any other member of this class.

3.5 Identity Independence

Another alternative conception of ontological dependence starts with an entity's identity. Here we must distinguish two notions of identity. First, every entity bears a *relation of identity* to itself alone; for any x, $x = x$. Second, for some entities there is a fact of the matter as to which entities they are, or to be more precise, which entities of their kind they are. For instance, there is a fact of the matter as to which person I am, and as to which event was the event of my birth. Let us term identity in this sense (in the sense of there being this fact of the matter) an entity's *individual identity*.

While every entity bears the relation of identity to itself, there may be entities that are *non-individuals*; that is, entities that can be differentiated from each other, but where there is no fact of the matter as to which is which. One possible example of non-individuals is provided by electrons in an entangled state. If electron x and electron y are in such a state, each will have a direction of spin opposite to that of the other. This difference entails that x is not identical with y. However, there is no fact of the matter as to which direction of spin each electron has. Therefore, it is at least possible that there is no fact of the matter as to which electron is which, and so it is possible that they are non-individuals (Lowe 2016). The conception of ontological dependence I shall presently outline (identity-dependence) concerns only entities with individual identities; likewise, I assume that substances are individuals.[15]

Given the notion of individual identity we can now characterise a sense in which an entity depends for its identity on other entities. Informally put, 'to say that the identity of x depends on the identity of y – or, more briefly, that

---

[14] It is worth noting that on alternative characterisations of natural numbers, such as mathematical structuralism (see Section 6.1), the problem Koslicki describes arguably does not arise.

[15] The distinction between individuals and non-individuals is different to that between particulars and universals. I assume that a universal can in principle have multiple instances, and a particular cannot. If there are non-individuals they can be particulars, and many (perhaps all) universals are individuals in the sense that there is a fact of the matter as to which universal is which.

x depends for its identity upon *y* – is to say that *which* thing of its kind *y* is fixes (or at least helps to fix) *which* thing of its kind *x* is. By "fixes" in this context is meant *metaphysically determines*' (Tahko & Lowe 2020, section 4.2). For instance, the individual identity of a non-empty set, which set it is, is determined by the identities of its members. So a non-empty set will depend for its identity on the identity of each of its members, and the identity of this set will be fully determined by the identities of all of its members together. We can formulate this kind of dependence as follows: *x* is *identity-dependent* on *y* =$_{def}$ necessarily, the identity of *x* is determined in part by the identity of *y* (for slightly different formulations, see Lowe 1998, 147–9; Tahko and Lowe 2020, section 4.2).

While identity-dependence is similar to essential dependence, they differ in certain respects. Unlike essential dependence, identity-dependence is necessarily rigid. If *x*'s identity is determined in part by the identity of *y*, *x* rigidly depends upon *y*; it is the identity of *y* specifically, and not any entity like *y*, which plays the role of determining *x*'s identity. Identity-dependence also entails rigid existential dependence: if *x* depends for its identity on *y*, then necessarily, if *x* exists *y* exists (Lowe 1998, 149–50; for criticism of this claim, see Correia 2005, 51–3; for a response, see Lowe 2013, 201–3). In contrast, it seems possible for some entities to essentially depend upon non-existent entities. Consider a dispositional property (e.g., *being soluble*). It seems essential to this property that it dispose its bearer to dissolve in liquid. But it is also plausible that an entity can have this disposition in a universe with no liquid. That is, while liquid features in the essence of the property *being soluble*, it seems possible that this property can be instantiated in the absence of any liquid (see also Wang 2019, 47–8).

Identity-dependence allows us to define another Independence Criterion:

> Identity Independence Criterion (IIC): *x* is a substance =$_{def}$ there is no entity *y* such that *x* depends for its identity on the identity of *y* (Lowe 1998, 151).

Like EIC, IIC avoids many of the problems facing REIC and GEIC (151–3). It is compatible with substances necessarily belonging to sets, necessarily having certain properties or certain parts, and with necessarily existing entities. In at least some respects, it also seems to be an improvement on EIC. As noted earlier, if a complex entity such as a cat generically essentially depends on entities of a certain type (e.g., cells of a certain kind) then EIC seems to rule it out as a substance. But IIC does not rule out cats on these grounds, assuming (as seems plausible) that the identity of a specific cat is not determined (even in part) by the identity of any particular cell or cells.

That said, IIC does face counter-examples. First, it may not be a sufficient condition for substancehood, since it can seemingly be satisfied by entities that intuitively are not substances. Michael Gorman (2006, 113) gives the example of an orchestra, a musical ensemble that can survive changes in its membership and so does not depend for its identity on any of its members. Orchestras and other social groups do not seem suitable to count as substances, fundamental building blocks of reality. Gorman's own diagnosis is that they lack the right degree of unity (113; see also Section 5.3 of this Element).

Conversely, IIC threatens to rule out plausible candidate substances (these counter-examples, unlike the previous one, also apply to EIC). For instance, it rules out any entity with an essential part, such as a water molecule essentially composed of specific atoms (Gorman 2006, 114; see also Correia 2005, 133; Koslicki 2018, 170–1).[16] In addition, IIC would seem to rule out any entity essentially bearing a specific trope, since on the face of it the identity of such an entity would be determined by that of the trope. In response to this worry, Lowe (1998, 142–3, 152) suggests that such a trope would be identical with its bearer, or perhaps the bearer would be identical with all of its essential tropes. However, this would seem to undermine the categorical distinction that Lowe insists on elsewhere between substances and their tropes, where the latter are understood as 'particular "ways" individual substances are' (Lowe 1998, 208; see also Hoffman 2011, 501–2).

3.6 Categorical Independence

The different versions of Independence considered so far have all focused on individual substances as independent entities. But there is another way to develop Independence, in terms of the *category* substance enjoying a specific kind of independence. This kind of *categorical independence* has been developed in a number of works by Joshua Hoffman and Gary Rosenkrantz. In what follows, I shall discus the version of their account offered in their 1997 volume and later work.

Hoffman and Rosenkrantz (1997) begin with the notion of *ontological categories*, general kinds that divide up the world in ontologically important ways. They suggest that the most general categorical distinction is that between *abstract* and *concrete* entities (46–7). Roughly speaking, a concrete entity exists in space, time or both; an abstract entity exists in neither. Below this distinction lies a further level of categories, including universal properties, events, and collections. Entities belonging to categories at this level can be either abstract or concrete. Hoffman and Rosenkrantz term this level of categories level C.

---

[16] Lowe argues that IIC is compatible with substances having essential parts (1998, 151–2, n. 12); for criticism, see Correia 2005, 133 n. 49; Gorman 2006, 114–16; Hoffman 2011, 504.

Next, Hoffman and Rosenkrantz suggest that an entity x is *independent-within-its-kind* if it could be the sole instance of its level C category through an interval of time (50). The notion of independence-within-its-kind can be understood in terms of ideas introduced earlier: it is basically a version of generic existential dependence where the scope of what x is independent of is restricted to other entities of x's category during a certain interval (and where x must exist during that interval).

Hoffman and Rosenkrantz do not suggest that all substances must be independent in this way. But they use the notion of independence-within-its-kind to formulate a criterion of substancehood:

> Categorical Independence Criterion (CIC): 'x is a substance if and only if x is an instance of a level C category, $C1$, such that: (i) $C1$ could have a single instance throughout an interval of time, and (ii) $C1$'s instantiation does not entail the instantiation of *another* level C category which satisfies (i), and (iii) it is impossible that something belonging to $C1$ has as a part something belonging to *another* level C category (other than the categories of Concrete Proper Part and Abstract Proper Part).' (Hoffman & Rosenkrantz 2007, 132)

The idea is to use clauses (i)–(iii) to exclude various categories, so that *substance* is the only level C category that $C1$ could be. For instance, properties could not satisfy (i), at least on an abundant conception of properties (on which, roughly speaking, for each possible predicate there is a single corresponding property). On such a conception any property will instantiate the distinct property *being a property* (Hoffman & Rosenkrantz 1994, 127–8). The category of collection or sum does not satisfy (iii), since there can be collections that include entities from many level C categories (120). And many types of entities, such as sense data, are plausibly such that they cannot exist unless there are substances; such types would not satisfy (ii) (141).

Unlike the previous Independence criteria, objections to CIC have not focused on possible counter-examples but on alleged theoretical shortcomings. One objection is that CIC does not explain what unifies the category of substance; that is, given two candidate substances, what explains their belonging to a single category? As Penelope Mackie (2000, 151–2) puts it, 'given that there can be "dependent substances", what makes it true that they belong to the same level C category as independent substances?' (see also Toner 2011, 41–2; Robinson 2021, section 3.1). This is not an epistemic objection; the issue is not how we could be justified in claiming that two entities belong to the same category (Toner 2011, 42 n. 6). The issue is that the analysis does not provide a clear account of what it is for these entities to belong to the same category.

A possible answer to this objection is suggested in the following remark: 'necessarily, because Material Object is a *species* of Substance, if *some* material object is a substance, then *all* material objects are substances' (Hoffman & Rosenkrantz 2007, 140). But it is not clear why we should accept that the category Material Object is a species of the category Substance. It is at least open to us to say that both substances and non-substances can be material objects. It might follow from this that material objects do not together form a genuine ontological category, or at least do not form one that can fit into Hoffman and Rosenkrantz's categorical framework. But this is hardly unprecedented. There are many ways of grouping together entities in such a way that they do not form a single ontological category. For instance, 'mental entity', which includes mental properties, events, substances, and so on, would not be a single ontological category in Hoffman and Rosenkrantz's framework (consider also the discussion of natural numbers in Section 3.4).

Another possible objection concerns the adequacy of the proposed analysis. The thought is that Hoffman and Rosenkrantz have not told us what it is for an entity to be a substance; that is, it is not clear that x's being a substance is explained by its fulfilling CIC (even if it is true that all and only substances fulfil CIC).[17] For instance, consider CIC's condition (ii): for something to count as a substance, it must belong to a category that can be instantiated without requiring an instantiation of any other level C category that satisfies (i). This condition is compatible with an entity's counting as a substance even though the category to which it belongs cannot be instantiated unless many other level C categories are instantiated, provided that these other categories do *not* satisfy (i). One might ask why this difference is relevant to substancehood. Why is it that failing to be independent of any other level C category that meets (i) would disqualify an entity from substancehood, but failing to be independent of any other level C category that does not meet (i) would not? This question does not rule out CIC, but it does suggest that the proposed analysis stands in need of further defence.[18]

4 Criteria of Substancehood: Grounding and Explanation

4.1 Metaphysical Explanation and Grounding

Parallel to the recent renewal of interest in ontological dependence, metaphysicians have increasingly focused on *grounding* and *metaphysical explanation*. The literature on these topics (in particular on grounding – see Raven 2020) is

---

[17] Hoffman and Rosenkrantz assume that a successful analytical definition of substance must provide such an explanation (2007, 132–3).

[18] For discussion of further objections to CIC, see Schnieder 2005; Hoffman & Rosenkrantz 2007.

already large, and I shall not attempt to summarise it here. Rather, I shall sketch some relevant options for thinking about grounding and metaphysical explanation and consider ways in which these might provide criteria of substancehood.

The notion of *metaphysical explanation* is typically taken to be non-causal and illustrated by examples: for instance, a faculty meeting occurs because the faculty are gathered discussing matters of importance to the department (Dasgupta 2017, 75); a shirt is red in virtue of its being maroon (Audi 2012, 689); the truth of a statement is explained by the way some part or aspect of reality is (Schaffer 2010a, 35). In each of these cases, something exists or is a certain way in virtue of other things existing or being certain ways, where the phrase 'in virtue of' does not express a causal relation.[19]

Grounding is closely related to metaphysical explanation and is often illustrated by the same examples. On one view, grounding is a worldly relation or structure that metaphysical explanations track, in much the same way that causal relations are typically taken to track relations of causation (Audi 2012, 687–8).[20] On this interpretation of grounding, explanations are typically taken to be closely tied to our conceptual and epistemic interests and activities; we engage in the activity of explaining, and explanations are representations typically produced by such activity. On another view, grounding is identified with metaphysical explanation; for something to be grounded by something else just is for the first thing to be metaphysically explained by the second (Dasgupta 2017, 75). On this interpretation, explanations are usually taken to be themselves objective, in the sense of being relatively independent of our activities and interests (e.g., Correia 2008, 1021–2). So, for instance, facts or propositions would be explained by other facts or propositions, regardless of what anyone thinks about them. For an alternative approach on which grounding is identified with explanations that are not objective in this sense, see Thompson's (2018a) article; for further discussion, see Brenner and colleagues' (2021) outline.

Grounding is standardly taken to be irreflexive, asymmetric, transitive and non-monotonic. Furthermore, it is typically assumed that the full grounds of an entity metaphysically necessitate the existence of that entity. Almost all of these features have been questioned (e.g., for discussion of the formal features of grounding, see Thompson 2020). That said, they are each widely accepted and help to make up the current orthodox view of grounding. It is common to

---

[19] Strictly speaking not all entities exist: states of affairs obtain, events occur, and so on. For ease of presentation, I shall use 'exist' and its cognates to designate all of these different ways in which entities can help to make up reality.

[20] Grounding may be taken to be the only relation which such explanations track, or it may be taken to be one of a number of such relations (see Brenner et al. 2021, section 2).

assume that the relata of grounding relations are facts or propositions, but I shall speak more generally of entities as grounding or being grounded.

The notions of grounding and ontological dependence have often been closely linked in the literature, and occasionally treated as picking out the same relation (e.g., Schaffer 2009a, 373). However, I suggest that the basic ideas behind each are different, such that the first does not clearly entail the second. The basic idea underlying all forms of ontological dependence is that an entity requires something of other entities for its existence or identity, for example. Dependence goes from the dependent entity to what it depends upon. In contrast, the basic idea of grounding is that an entity or entities generate something else: they bring it about or make it the case that it exists or is a certain way (where this means at least that true grounding claims licence metaphysical explanations, of one thing's existing or being a certain way because other things exist or are certain ways). Grounding, on this view, goes from the grounds to what they explain. The grounds metaphysically determine what they ground, but this idea seems to leave open whether each grounded entity requires anything of any other entities in order to exist or be as it is.

The strength of this claim should not be overstated. There are some instances of grounding where plausibly the grounded entity does ontologically depend on its grounds (for instance, the existence of non-empty sets is often taken to be grounded in the existence of their members, and sets also ontologically depend on their members). Nor am I claiming that there are any instances of grounding where it is clear that the grounded entities are not ontologically dependent. My claim is the more modest one, that the basic idea of grounding is different to and does not obviously entail the basic idea of ontological dependence (for further discussion, see Schnieder 2020; Rydéhn 2021). So while it may turn out that a conception of substancehood in terms of grounding is closely related to or even entails a conception in terms of ontological dependence, one need not assume this at the outset.

4.2 Ungroundedness and Explanatory Independence

Equipped with a basic notion of grounding, we can define a criterion of substancehood:

Ungrounded Criterion (UC): x is a substance $=_{def}$ nothing grounds x.[21]

---

[21] This is Schaffer's (2009a, 373) definition of a fundamental entity. At various places he describes substances as the fundamental entities (e.g., Schaffer 2009a, 356, 376; though see Section 6.2). However, it is also possible to modify UC so that it would be a necessary condition rather than a definition of what it is for x to be a substance. This necessary condition would be informative in that it would spell out the intuitive idea that substances are fundamental entities (see Sections 1

A version of UC can also be formulated if grounding is restricted to holding between facts:

UC*: x is a substance $=_{def}$ nothing grounds the fact that x exists.[22]

A closely related criterion of substancehood is offered by Benjamin Schnieder. First, Schnieder introduces the notion of explanatory dependence:

> x *depends explanatorily* upon $y =_{def}$ necessarily, whenever x exists, it exists because y is F at that time. (Schnieder 2006, 412; see also Correia 2005, 70; 2008, 1020–3)

Thus stated, explanatory dependence is a rigid form of dependence, but a generic version can be formulated straightforwardly. As an example of explanatorily dependent entities Schnieder (2006, 409) mentions tropes, which 'exist because their bearers, or subjects, or hosts are thus-and-so'.

The explanations that Schnieder regards as relevant to explanatory dependence are *conceptual* (i.e., based on conceptual relations). The order of explanation is determined by the relative complexity of the relevant concepts: 'In general, statements involving complex or elaborated concepts are explained with recourse to more primitive concepts' (Schnieder 2006, 406). So, for example, in the case of tropes Schnieder argues that their 'canonical designators' (phrases such as 'Socrates's paleness') are complex expressions that express logically complex concepts; these are built out of and explained by simpler concepts (e.g., 'Socrates', 'pale'), which occur in the explanans ('Socrates is pale') (410–11). In this way, the existence of the trope *Socrates's paleness* is explained by Socrates being pale.

The notion of explanatory dependence can be used to formulate a criterion of substancehood:

> Explanatory Independence Criterion (ExIC): x is a substance $=_{def}$ there is no entity y such that x is explanatorily dependent upon y.[23] (adapted from Schnieder 2006, 412)

UC, UC*, and ExIC all appeal to the same basic idea that substances (or fundamental entities more generally) are not made to exist by anything else; for a given substance to exist, there is nothing else in virtue of which it exists (see also Bennett 2017, 105).

---

and 2.2) in a specific way (i.e., in terms of grounding). This point also applies to the criterion UC*, which I shall introduce presently.

[22] A possible complicating factor is that not at all grounding theorists accept that there are existence facts (e.g., Audi 2012, 700–1).

[23] While Schnieder offers a definition of substance, it is also possible to modify ExIC so that it states an informative necessary condition on substancehood (following n. 21).

This idea is compatible with substances existentially depending, both rigidly and generically, on other entities. Whether it is also compatible with a substance's depending on something else for its essence or its identity is more controversial. But at any rate it is not obvious that an unground entity cannot be essentially dependent or identity-dependent.

Furthermore, UC, UC*, and ExIC each suggest a role that substances can play: that of together metaphysically explaining everything else that exists (see n. 7). Taking UC as an example, one might claim that anything that is not a substance is itself grounded in a substance or substances. This claim is not entailed by UC (nor is an equivalent claim entailed by either UC* or ExIC). But together with any of these criteria, such claims would capture the sense in which substances are 'unexplained explainers': unexplained because they are not grounded or explanatorily dependent, explainers in that together they ground or explain all else (Bennett 2017, 111).

4.3 Assessing the Criteria

There are a number of lines of criticism that might be aimed at these proposals. To start with, various criticisms have been levelled at grounding (see Koslicki 2020; for defence of grounding, see deRossett 2020; for further discussion of whether substancehood can be characterised using the notion of grounding, see Koslicki 2015; Raven 2017).

The details of Schnieder's conception of explanatory dependence are also open to question. It is far from clear that all non-causal explanations are conceptual explanations as Schnieder characterises the latter. For instance, the following seems possible: mental facts are metaphysically explained by physical facts, but this explanation can only be known or understood a posteriori. Such an explanation seems very different to the kinds of examples offered by Schnieder (2006, 403), which exploit conceptual links that are available a priori.

Furthermore, it is unclear why we should expect that the order of metaphysical explanation would always proceed from the conceptually more simple to the more complex (Koslicki 2018, 148–9). Take the example of the trope *Socrates's paleness*, the existence of which is supposed to be explained by Socrates's being pale. A trope theorist may deny that there is any universal property *being pale*. So it is not clear why this theorist would be forced to explain the existence of this trope by appeal to Socrates's being pale, since it not clear that the phrase 'Socrates is pale' picks out anything in virtue of which this trope exists. Alternatively, one might argue that Socrates's being pale is explained by this trope's inhering in Socrates; perhaps for an entity to be pale is for it to belong to a certain resemblance class in virtue of its having a paleness trope. Either way, the order of metaphysical explanation does not seem to track the conceptual order in the way Schnieder assumes.[24]

In addition to this worry, ExIC faces possible counter-examples (which also seem to apply to UC and UC*). For instance, there are entities the existence of which plausibly cannot be explained but which many regard as doubtful candidates to be substances, such as the empty set or simple Platonic universals (Correia 2005, 129). Correia suggests that these examples can be dealt with by limiting candidate substances to concrete entities (130). Correia also worries that a proposal very like ExIC would exclude as a substance any entity with essential proper parts (128). Whether or not ExIC would rule out such entities would depend on whether the existence of such entities is metaphysically explained by their essential proper parts. As mentioned briefly in Section 4.2, it is not clear whether or not an entity must be grounded in the entities on which it essentially depends; nor is it clear whether its existence can be metaphysically explained, even in part, by appeal to those other entities.

Setting possible counter-examples aside, we may still wonder how the proposals on the table (UC, UC*, and ExIC) are supposed to work. The basic idea that they each express – that the existence of substances does not require explanation – is promising at least as a necessary condition on substancehood, but the notions of metaphysical explanation or grounding that underlie them stand in need of further development. In Section 4.4, I shall sketch one way in which this might proceed, focusing on grounding.

4.4 Developing the Criteria

One way to think of grounding is as a primitive relation that does not admit of varieties (Schaffer 2009a, 376–7; Audi 2012, 688–9). This view is compatible with either UC or UC*. However, if grounding is understood in this way, it is not clear how either UC or UC* take us beyond the intuitive idea outlined in the previous paragraph, that substances are such that their existence does not require explanation. It would be preferable if we could say something more about grounding and the correlative criterion of substancehood as being ungrounded.

A different approach admits different kinds of grounding. For instance, one might think of 'grounding' as an umbrella term for a variety of more determinate metaphysical relations (e.g., realisation, composition, set formation, and perhaps others). Understood in this way, the notion of grounding would be

---

[24] In response to similar criticisms Schnieder (2020) suggests that proponents of explanatory dependence should reject the specific trope theories described in the main text (112 n. 30). But this response seems to miss the deeper problem that the order of metaphysical explanation may not always track the conceptual order.

similar to Karen Bennett's (2007, 12) notion of 'building relations'.[25] There are various ways in which one might think that these more determinate relations all belong together in a unified class. Bennett claims that each of these determinate relations is directed (i.e., asymmetrical), and is such that the 'builders' generate and metaphysically necessitate what they build (60). By 'generate', Bennett means that each building relation is apt to be appealed to in a metaphysical explanation. That is, one could answer the question 'Why does x exist?', with a statement of the form 'Because x is composed of Ys arranged in such-and-such a way', or 'Because x is a non-empty set and its members, some Ys, exist'. Exactly which statement of this form would be the right answer would depend on what kind of entity x is; but if the question can be answered by some such statement, then x is grounded and the statement would indicate what it is that grounds it.

A different view of grounding as admitting varieties is that it is a genus with different species; the determination relations just listed (composition, realisation, etc.) are not the species of the genus but the differentia, the features that distinguish the different species of grounding. For instance, grounding might be a relation between facts, and we can distinguish between those instances of grounding that involve composition (e.g., facts about x are grounded in facts about Ys, where x is composed of Ys) from those that involve realisation (e.g., facts about x's being F are grounded in facts about x's being G, where instances of F are realised by instances of G), and so on.[26]

On either of these views of grounding, UC would in effect become a claim like the following:

> UC': x is a substance $=_{\text{def}}$ nothing composes x, and nothing realises x, and . . .
> (for a similar view see Bennett 2017, 105–6)

I have formulated UC' using an open-ended list to accommodate the possibility that entities can be metaphysically explained by reference to determinate relations not listed. Because of this it might be thought that UC' is not so much a concrete criterion of substancehood as a guideline for further investigation.

There are further issues with UC'. In particular, there are disputes as to which determinate relations really underwrite metaphysical explanations, and in which direction those explanations run. For example, it is typically assumed that the existence of wholes is explained by the existence and arrangement of

---

[25] Something like this idea is also found in Kelly Trogdon's (2018) discussion of *grounding mechanisms*: 'determination relations of a certain sort holding between constituents of grounding facts and constituents of the facts they ground' (1290).

[26] Another view holds that 'grounding' is an umbrella term but that there is in fact no substantive unity among the different determinate relations that fall under it (Wilson 2014; Koslicki 2015). For further discussion of the unity of grounding, see Richardson 2020.

their parts, but it has been claimed that at least some wholes explain the existence of their parts (Schaffer 2010a).

Nevertheless, UC' is worth taking seriously. It takes us beyond the intuitive idea on which UC, UC*, and ExIC are each based, that the existence of substances does not admit of explanation. It does so by articulating the relevant notion of metaphysical explanation in terms of different metaphysical relations that might be thought to underwrite such explanations.

5 Further Criteria of Substancehood

5.1 Ultimate Subject

In this section, I shall consider three further approaches to substancehood. The first of these is thinking of substances as *ultimate subjects*. Characterised in this way, substances can be contrasted with entities that have an *adjectival mode of being*, entities that are modifications or qualifications of other entities or are in some sense constituted by such modifications. Entities with adjectival modes of being, or adjectival entities, include *properties*, *relations*, *states* (e.g., the state of being dented or of forming a fist), at least some *events* (e.g., Amy's smiling), and entities constituted by other entities being in certain states or undergoing certain events (e.g., a particular dent, or Amy's smile).[27]

An ultimate subject is not an adjectival entity; it is not itself a modification of anything else, nor is it constituted by something else (or some other things) being modified in any way.[28] It is something that, as Peter Van Inwagen (1993, 23) puts it, exists 'in its own right', as opposed to existing in something else's right as, for instance, a mere modification of that other entity. The Ultimate Subject criterion of substancehood is the claim that necessarily, a substance is an ultimate subject.

While the notion of an adjectival entity is somewhat vague, it does seem possible to give examples of entities that are clearly not adjectival. Consider an organism such as a cat. Plausibly, for a cat to exist certain cells must be arranged in a certain way. One might say that for the cells to be arranged in this way is for them to be collectively qualified or modified. But plausibly the cat is not constituted by this arrangement of cells in anything like the way in which a dent is constituted by something's being dented. For instance, the cat could

---

[27] In this context, properties and relations can be understood as either particulars (i.e., tropes) or as universals on an Aristotelian conception, on which universals only exist if they are instantiated. On the rival Platonic conception, universals can exist uninstantiated (on the distinction between these conceptions, see Loux 2006, 40–3). It is more difficult to understand Platonic properties or relations as adjectival entities.

[28] For versions of this characterisation, see Van Inwagen 1993, 22–23; Shoemaker 1997, 287; Simons 1998, 237; Heil 2003, 179; Broackes 2006, 137; Olson 2007, 5.

have been constituted by different cells to those that actually make it up, whereas plausibly a particular dent could not have been constituted by some other entity's being dented. The cat, one is tempted to say, is something over and above the cells that actually compose it being arranged in a certain way, whereas the dent is nothing over and above a particular entity's being dented (see also Olson 2007, 134–5).

I have introduced Ultimate Subject as an alternative to Independence, but the former criterion has often been regarded as a version of the latter (e.g., Ayers 1991, 70; Simons 1998, 237; Koslicki 2018, 140). The thought is that adjectival entities are dependent on other, modified entities; an ultimate subject, in contrast, is not dependent in this way. It is plausible that Ultimate Subject entails some version of Independence, but it is not obvious that understanding the first as a version of the second fully captures the thought that substances are ultimate subjects. What seems distinctive about Ultimate Subject is that it aims to clarify what it is to be a substance by reference to a specific contrast class of non-substances (adjectival entities) that are grouped together because they exist in a certain way. To say that an entity has an adjectival mode of being is to tie it to some other entity or entities in a quite specific way: what that entity is, is a modification or qualification of something else (or it is constituted by such a modification). An ultimate subject is not tied to any other entity in this specific way, even if it turns out that some ultimate subjects are themselves ontologically dependent. (That said, those who regard the notion of being an ultimate subject as designating a kind of independence can interpret Ultimate Subject as a version of Independence or as falling under one of the versions of Independence already discussed.)[29]

One objection to Ultimate Subject is that it involves reading an ontological distinction off of a pre-existing linguistic or conceptual one. The worry here is that this involves illegitimately projecting categories and distinctions from thought or language onto the world, without a good reason to think that how reality is will match how we happen to think or talk about it. It is historically true that metaphysicians have often relied on linguistic or conceptual categories to generate ontological categories. It is also true that this approach to metaphysics has come under severe criticism, for instance from John Heil (2003).

However, Ultimate Subject need not be understood as simply importing a linguistic or conceptual distinction into ontology. The contrast between

---

[29] Hoffman and Rosenkrantz argue that what is substantially the Ultimate Subject criterion is not an Independence criterion (1994, 35–44). However, they interpret the latter in terms of asymmetric existential dependence, whereas if Ultimate Subject is to be understood as a species of Independence, it is more plausibly interpreted as involving some other kind of dependence, for example essential dependence.

ultimate subjects and adjectival entities can be illustrated by appealing to paradigmatic examples from either side (e.g., an individual horse versus this horse's state of being brown), and considering what the examples on either side have in common. This procedure does not seem on the face of it to require tracking existing linguistic categories (e.g., nouns or adjectives). Nor need it require tracking concepts that we already had prior to distinguishing between ultimate subjects and adjectival entities. (Of course, to draw this ontological distinction requires using concepts such as 'ultimate subject' and 'adjectival entity'. My point is that we do not have to understand this procedure as starting with a conceptual distinction that was already in hand and using this as a basis for drawing or recognising the ontological distinction.)

Let us move on to consider two further objections to thinking of substances as ultimate subjects. Each of these begins with the following observation: to think of x as an ultimate subject requires thinking of x as distinct from any entities that qualify or modify it, or that are constituted by x's being modified in some way (hereafter I will simply speak of x's properties, setting aside other entities that are adjectival upon x). The first objection is that the very idea of an entity distinct from any of its properties is incoherent. We can only have an idea of something by thinking of it as having some features or other. Therefore, strictly speaking it is impossible to think of any entity as an ultimate subject. The second objection is that even if the very idea of an entity distinct from its properties is coherent, there can be no entity corresponding to this idea. This is because no entity can exist without any properties. Bertrand Russell (1945, 201) expresses the worry like this: 'A substance is supposed to be the subject of properties, and to be something distinct from all its properties. But when we take away the properties, and try to imagine the substance by itself, we find that there is nothing left.'. That is, there can be no such entity as a propertyless or so-called bare particular or bare substratum.

I suggest that both of these objections rest on a misconception of substances as ultimate subjects. I shall address the second objection first. In thinking of x as an ultimate subject we must conceptually distinguish between x and all of its properties, but this does not entail that x could exist without having any properties. Consider a cat, Tibbles:

> Tibbles has properties (as all agree); and he is *distinct from* his properties, in the sense that he is *not identical with* any or all of them . . . But that does not imply that Tibbles and his properties are *separable*, in the sense that each could be *detached* from the other (leaving the subject without properties, and the properties without a subject). (Broackes 2006, 149)

The thought that an entity could exist without having any properties whatsoever is dubious in the extreme (e.g., Hoffman & Rosenkrantz 1997, 18; though see Sider 2006, 392–4). If properties are understood as ways that entities are or could be, an entity without any properties would seem to be an entity that exists in no way whatsoever.[30] For this reason, I am leery of any view of substances as what would be left over if all the properties belonging to an entity (Tibbles, say) were 'subtracted' from it.[31] But fortunately, the notion of a substance as an entity *distinct* from any of its properties does not require us to think of substances as *lacking* (or as capable of lacking) any property whatsoever.

The second objection, to which I have just responded, rests on an illicit move from *x* being distinct from its properties to *x* existing without any properties (or being capable of existing without any properties). The first objection rests on a similar move, from the concept of an entity that is distinct from any properties to the concept of an entity devoid of all properties. In response to this objection, note first that these are different concepts. As David Wiggins (2016, 54) puts it, the *bare idea of a subject* (thinking of *x* simply as something that bears properties, without specifying what those properties are) is one thing; the *idea of a bare subject* (thinking of *x* as something that has no properties) is quite another. When this distinction is clarified, it should also be clear that the first of these does not entail the second. The bare idea of a subject simply involves thinking of an entity as a property-bearer, abstracting from or setting aside the specific properties it bears or that it must bear. This does not require thinking of that entity as lacking all properties. And once this point is made, it is not clear what reason there might be to think that the bare idea of a subject is incoherent.[32]

Ultimate Subject indicates an important point: adjectival entities by and large seem poor candidates to be substances. So it is a reasonable necessary condition on substancehood that no substance can be an adjectival entity. If the distinction between ultimate subjects and adjectival entities is exhaustive (that is, if any entity whatsoever must be one or the other), Ultimate Subject would be plausible. That said, it is limited in an important respect. Consider sets, mereological

---

[30] That said, this line of thought would be rejected by proponents of austere realism, the view according to which there are no such entities as properties, be they particulars or universals (Loux 2006, 52).

[31] Thanks to a referee for this wording, and for encouraging me to address this suggestion.

[32] One might want to distinguish the idea of a bare or propertyless substratum from David Armstrong's idea of a *thin particular*, a particular (e.g., Tibbles) considered in abstraction from its non-relational properties (on this distinction, see Robinson 2021, section 3.2.2; on thin particulars, see Armstrong 1997, 123–5). If one accepts the notion of a thin particular, it may be possible to regard many objects as composed of (and so ontologically secondary to) a thin particular and properties. However, it is also possible to reject this idea. In particular, substance ontologists need not regard substances as either thin particulars or as combinations of thin particulars and properties.

sums, or social entities such as orchestras. As mentioned in Section 3, it is not clear that these entities are substances. But nor is it obvious that they are adjectival entities: at any rate, they do not clearly belong to one of the types of adjectival entities mentioned at the start of this sub-section (for further examples, see Van Inwagen 1993, 24–5; Crane 2003, 238). So even if being an ultimate subject is a necessary condition for being a substance, it is not clear whether it is sufficient.

5.2 Simplicity

Another proposed criterion of substancehood is Simplicity: necessarily, substances are simple entities. More precisely, an entity counts as a substance only if it has no *substantial parts*, proper parts that are themselves substances (Oderberg 2007, 80; Toner 2008, 287; Heil 2012, 4; Schaffer 2013, 83; Inman 2018, 103). Substantial parts can be contrasted with spatial parts and temporal parts. A *spatial part* of an entity is a portion of that entity which occupies a certain region of space (e.g., the top half of an apple). Likewise, a *temporal part* of an entity is a portion that occupies a certain extent or slice of time (e.g., my desk during 2021).

Simplicity is often taken to be compatible with substances having spatial or temporal parts (Heil 2012, 19). The basic idea is that substantial parts stand to the wholes to which they belong in a different way in which temporal or spatial parts do. Heil draws this difference in terms of whether or not the parts make up the wholes. An entity with substantial parts is composed from or made up of such parts; in contrast, an entity with spatial or temporal parts is not composed from those parts (Heil 2012, 34–5; see also Lowe 1998, 162; 2012, 99–100). One way to develop this distinction is in terms of essence or real definition.[33] For instance, if x has spatial parts, each of these parts will be defined precisely as a certain portion of x, whereas x cannot be defined as the collection of these parts (Lowe 1998, 115–17). In contrast, if x contains substantial entities as proper parts, these entities will not be defined as parts of x. For each of these entities, its essence is independent of its being a part of x. It is because they are independent of x in this way that they can be said to make x up, as opposed to their being carved out of x in the way that x's spatial parts are.

One argument for Simplicity is based on the thought that it is hard to see how a complex of substances could itself bear a property (Heil 2012, 21). It is true that the complex can be said to be various ways (e.g., to have a certain spatial extension).

---

[33] An alternative approach would be to appeal to the distinction drawn by Schaffer (2010a, 47–8) between *mere aggregates* and *integrated wholes* (for comparison, see Heil's discussion of line segments at 2012, 40–2).

But this kind of talk should not be taken as entailing that the complex itself bears properties. Rather, the complex being various ways is a matter of how its constituents are arranged and which properties they have.

Heil (2012, 151–78) develops this idea in terms of *truth-making*. Consider a complex entity such as a cat. We can make various true statements about this cat: it has a specific height, colour, and so on. Heil suggests that what makes these statements true is not the cat itself bearing properties, but the properties of the cat's substantial parts and how those parts are arranged (23–4, 286–7). So, for instance, what makes it true that the cat has a certain height is that its parts are arranged in such a way that together they have a certain spatial extension along a given axis.[34]

There are various issues with this line of thought. First, it is misleading to characterise each entity with substantial parts as a complex of substances, at least insofar as this characterisation suggests that each such entity is identical with some specific collection of specific substances.[35] Many candidate complex substances seem to be distinct from the collection of their specific parts. For instance, an organism such as a cat is composed of cells, but it is incorrect to identify a cat with the specific collection of cells that actually compose it, since that very cat could have been composed of different cells and can survive the replacement of some of the cells that compose it.

Given this, it would be premature to assume that any way the complex entity can be said to be is just a matter of the properties of its substantial parts and how these parts are arranged. For instance, one true statement we can make about the cat is that it can survive the replacement of some or all of its substantial parts. But this is not true of the specific collection of the parts that make it up. Consequently, it is not clear how its parts, even arranged in a specific way, could make this statement about the cat true.

Schaffer presents two different arguments for Simplicity. The first of these is the *argument from economy*. To outline this argument, we must first introduce the notion of *completeness*: 'a plurality of entities is complete if and only if duplicating all these entities, while preserving their fundamental relations, metaphysically suffices to duplicate the cosmos and its contents' (Schaffer 2010a, 39). Schaffer holds that not only should the fundamental entities taken together be complete, but that they should be '*minimally*

---

[34] It does not follow that truths about the cat can be translated or analysed into truths about its parts (Heil 2012, 6). Truthmaker theory is usually thought to be compatible with there being no such analysis or translation.

[35] That is, the collection of the particular substances each of which is a substantial part of the whole. The key point is that this very collection rigidly depends on each of its members and cannot survive their loss or replacement (Heil 2012, 34). Nor could this very collection have been composed of different substances.

complete, in having no proper subplurality that is complete' (40). If some substances include others as parts, this would violate minimal completeness: 'any complete plurality of fundamentals that includes a whole and one of its proper parts will have a complete subplurality without this proper part, and so fail to be minimal' (41).

Schaffer claims that the fundamental entities should together be minimally complete because if they were not, some of them would be redundant. But whether or not certain candidate fundamental entities are redundant will depend on which roles they are supposed to play. One such role is that of being the *fundamental base* from which all else arises. Following Schaffer, let us think of this role in terms of *grounding*: the fundamental base consists of those entities each of which is ungrounded and that together ground everything else (2009a, 351; see Section 4.2 of this Element). It does seem crucial to this role that fixing the entities that together make up the fundamental base will thereby fix every-thing else; completeness is a way of acknowledging this.

Now suppose that a sub-section of the fundamental base, S, was itself complete. Schaffer would argue that in that case the entities in the fundamental base that were not in S would be redundant. But this does not follow. Completeness is defined in terms of metaphysical necessitation, whereas the theoretical role of being a part of the fundamental base is defined in terms of grounding. And while grounding is standardly thought to entail metaphysical necessitation, the reverse is plausibly not true. An entity x could metaphysically necessitate another entity y without grounding it (think of the existence of {Socrates} necessitating that of Socrates). Therefore, the members of S could together metaphysically necessitate every entity not in the fundamental base without thereby grounding every such entity. So considerations of theoretical economy do not by themselves entail that the fundamental base is minimally complete (for a similar criticism of Schaffer, see Bennett 2017, 109).

It might be suggested that the argument from economy could be rescued if completeness is defined not in modal terms, but in terms of grounding or Bennett's (2017, 109) notion of building relations (see Section 4.4).[36] For instance, one might say that the Xs are complete at world w iff the Xs individually or together ground everything else at w. And the Xs are minim-ally complete iff they are complete and there is no subset of the Xs, the Ys, which are also complete.

Given these definitions, it does seem plausible that the fundamental entities at a world must be minimally complete. However, it is not clear that given these definitions the fundamentalia could not include complex entities some of whose

---

[36] Thanks to an anonymous referee for suggesting that I consider this possibility.

proper parts are also fundamental (e.g., ungrounded entities that help to ground everything else). For all that has been said so far, it may be that there are complex entities such that neither the complex entities ground their proper parts, nor do the parts ground the complex entities (I shall discuss this possibility in more detail later in this sub-section). It is not clear why including such complex entities among the fundamentalia would necessitate that minimal completeness would be violated. That is, if there are such complex entities among the fundamentalia, it is not clear that there must be a subset of fundamental entities that includes the parts but not the wholes and that is itself complete; nor is it clear that there must be a subset of fundamental entities that includes the wholes but not the parts and that is complete.[37] And if the inclusion of complex entities among the fundamentalia does not necessitate a violation of minimal completeness, the argument from economy will not work.

Schaffer's (2010a) second argument for Simplicity is the *argument from recombinability*. This argument relies on the premise that 'the fundamental actual concrete objects should be *freely recombinable*, serving as independent units of being' (40). Very roughly, two entities are freely recombinable with each other if the intrinsic properties had by one do not metaphysically necessitate anything about the intrinsic properties had by the other (for more detail, see Schaffer 2010b, 350–5). Entities that stand in part–whole relations to each other (or indeed that mereologically overlap at all) are not freely recombinable (355). Therefore, no fundamental entity can be a proper part of another fundamental entity.

This argument is vulnerable to a similar objection as that leveled at the argument from economy. Free recombination is a modal condition. If metaphysical necessitation and grounding can come apart, it may be that distinct entities can modally constrain each other without standing in grounding relations to each other. Indeed, it is not clear why they could not modally constrain each other even if each is ungrounded. More generally, it is not obvious why fundamental entities must be freely recombinable; on the face of it, this does not

---

[37] The crucial difference with Schaffer's original formulation of the argument is as follows: in the original formulation, a complex entity will have properties that determine the intrinsic properties and relations holding between the parts (2010a, 41). Because of this, if the fundamentalia include a complex entity, the properties of that entity would metaphysically necessitate that its parts have certain intrinsic properties and stand in certain relations, and so any complete plurality of fundamentals that includes a whole and its parts would have a complete sub-plurality that did not include the parts. This argument presupposes that completeness is understood modally. If completeness is understood non-modally (e.g., in terms of grounding) and if not all proper parts are grounded in the wholes to which they belong, then it is not true that any plurality of fundamentals that includes a whole but none of its proper parts would necessarily be complete.

follow from their status as fundamental (e.g., as together forming the fundamental base – for further discussion, see Wang 2016).

These responses to Schaffer's arguments rely on the assumption that it is possible for metaphysical necessitation to hold without grounding relations. This assumption has been questioned on theoretical grounds. The idea is that in general it is better to explain modal co-variation by appeal to grounding relations than to treat it as brute. So if x and y are distinct entities that modally constrain each other, we are entitled to infer that either x grounds y, y grounds x, or both x and y are grounded by some further entity or entities (Ismael & Schaffer 2019, 4135–9). But even if it is better to explain modal co-variation than to treat it as brute, other ways of explaining it may be available. For instance, one might try to explain x and y's modally constraining each other by appealing to essential relations holding between them (Calosi & Morganti 2020). It may be possible that distinct fundamental entities are essentially related and thus modally constrain each other without grounding each other. (This would rule out such entities counting as substances on EIC, but it might be compatible with other criteria of substancehood, such as IIC or UC.)

So far I have considered arguments in favour of Simplicity. There are fewer arguments against it. Many philosophers who reject Simplicity appeal to paradigmatic substances that are standardly understood as complex (e.g., molecules or organisms).[38] This of course takes us back to the first methodological issue outlined in Section 3.1: to what extent can we rely on such paradigms to determine our conception of substancehood? Both Heil and Schaffer adopt revisionary views about such examples, holding that in the final analysis they do not count as substances.[39]

Another way to argue against Simplicity would be to spell out a conception of complex entities that allows at least some of them to satisfy some of the criteria of substancehood outlined earlier. In the rest of this sub-section, I shall sketch one such conception, working with a notion of substances as entities whose existence is not metaphysically explained (i.e., ExIC from Section 4.2, although this notion could also be spelled out in terms of UC* or UC').

One might accept that some composite entities exist because their parts exist and are arranged in specific ways, but deny that this is true of all composite entities. On this view, some composite entities have parts, and perhaps could not exist without having parts, but they are not generated from their parts in such

---

[38] Schnieder (2006) goes further, assuming that any entity that is solely composed of substances is itself a substance. On this conception, 'portions of liquid, societies, and planetary systems will qualify as complex substances' (394).

[39] An alternative response is to deny that paradigmatically composite substances have substantial parts; see the discussion of Ross Inman's approach in Section 5.3.

a way that one could explain the existence of these composites by appealing to their parts and how they are arranged. Rory Madden (2015, 87) puts a similar point as follows: 'It is optional to explain what ordinary objects fundamentally *are* in terms of their composition from parts.' Madden suggests an alternative conception of some composite objects in terms of their activities and dispositions, which can be captured in lawlike generalisations. On this *nomological conception*, 'The metaphysically basic characterization of an ordinary kind of object states the lawlike activity of things of that kind' (Madden 2015, 87). Madden puts things in terms of the metaphysically basic characterisation of an entity, but it is reasonable to infer from this that the existence of such an entity (an entity whose basic characterisation is in terms of lawlike activities) cannot be explained by the existence and arrangement of its parts.[40]

One way to think of such entities is as *emergent complex substances*: given certain entities of certain kinds, the Ys, arranged in certain way, it is nomologically necessary that a further entity x will exist and include some or all of the Ys as parts, but the existence of x cannot be metaphysically explained by the Ys or their arrangement (for comparison, see McGinn 2000; O'Connor & Jacobs 2003; Jaworski 2016, 104). The fact that x is nomologically but not metaphysically determined by the Ys suggests it is a strongly ontologically emergent entity (compare with Van Cleve 1990, 222). That the existence of x cannot be explained by the Ys or their arrangement suggests that it is a substance, at least on ExIC. Alternatively, one might suggest that while the existence of x does consist in there being some Ys arranged in a certain way, for this specific arrangement to obtain just is for the Ys to compose an entity of the kind to which x belongs (where this might be an entity with certain characteristic properties or powers). In this way, any attempt to explain the existence of x by appeal to how certain Ys are arranged would seem to be circular. A possible (though by no means uncontroversial) example is a multi-cellular organism. It is very plausible that such an organism is composed of cells arranged in a certain way, but it may be that this arrangement cannot be specified without appealing to the cells belonging to an organism (or an organism of a certain kind). For instance, it may be that this arrangement cannot be specified without appealing to the cells together composing an entity with properties or powers that only living organisms possess. If that is the case, then multi-cellular organisms would seem to be good candidates to be emergent complex substances.

---

[40] An alternative account of the difference between composite entities that are generated from their parts and composites that are not so generated is developed by Inman (2018). See Section 5.3 of this Element.

5.3 Unity

The final criterion of substancehood I shall consider is Unity. I understand Unity as a necessary condition: x is a substance only if the proper parts or components of x are unified in a certain way. (For recent statements of Unity, see Ayers 1991, 72; Crane 2003, 242; Gorman 2006, 114; Schaffer 2013, 68; Inman 2018, 98; Koslicki 2018, 191.)[41]

I stated Unity in terms of 'parts or components' to cover cases where an entity in some sense contains or is composed of entities that intuitively are not among its proper parts. There is at least one view, hylomorphism, that is often understood in terms of substances being compounds of components (matter and substantial form) that are not proper parts of the substances they make up (Rea 2011, 342; Jaworski 2016, 327–8; Marmodoro 2021, 284–5; for defence of the claim that matter and substantial form are proper parts of substances, see Koslicki 2008, 176–86). That said, in what follows, for reasons of simplicity, I shall refer only to 'parts' rather than 'parts or components'.

At first glance Unity and Simplicity may seem to be different or even rival criteria of substancehood, since Unity relies tacitly on the assumption that the substances that satisfy it have proper parts. But Simplicity does not entail that substances cannot have proper parts; it only entails that they cannot have *substantial* proper parts. So in principle there may be composite entities that satisfy both Unity and Simplicity; they would have proper parts that are not themselves substances and that are unified in the appropriate way. Indeed, as we shall later see this is precisely the option taken by Inman.

Unity raises issues to do with composition, especially the Special Composition Question (roughly, when do various entities together compose a further entity?) (Van Inwagen 1990, 21–2). The most straightforward answers to this question are 'Never' and 'Always'. The proponent of a Unity criterion could accept 'Always' (i.e., unrestricted mereological composition), but in that case will probably want to distinguish between those composite entities that count as substances and those that do not. Alternatively, she may hold that composition is restricted, in that entities can together compose a further object in certain circumstances but not in others; if she takes this route she would be free to argue that all composite objects are in fact substances. Either way, I assume that the proponent of Unity accepts *restricted substantial composition* (only certain entities in certain circumstances can be unified so that they form a whole which is a substance).

---

[41] Unfortunately I will not be able to address many accounts of substantial unity (e.g., Hoffman & Rosenkrantz 1997; Kronen & Tuttle 2011) and much recent work on hylomorphism (e.g., Oderberg 2007; Koslicki 2008; Rea 2011; Jaworski 2016; Marmodoro 2021).

In what follows, I shall consider two different ways in which substantial composition might be restricted. First, it might be that the entities that make up the whole must be *arranged* or *configured* in a certain way, typically by being tightly bound together. One way to develop this idea is by positing relations of dependence holding between the parts; and it is tempting to appeal to one or more of the relations of ontological dependence discussed in Section 3. However, this does not seem satisfactory for at least some plausible candidate composite substances such as molecules (Koslicki 2018, 206–7).

Koslicki proposes an alternative way of understanding the required configuration among the parts, that of *lawful interactional dependence*:

> an integrated whole derives its unity from the way in which its parts are able to interact with other parts of the same whole; the interplay between these activities carried out by the parts of an integral whole in turn allows the whole as well to manifest certain of its capacities, namely, those whose manifestation by the whole requires 'team work' among its parts. (210).

Roughly, the idea is that each part has some causal capacities, the manifestation of which requires that capacities belonging to other parts of the same whole also manifest themselves (211–12). As an example of this kind of dependence, Koslicki describes the interactions between the parts of a Philips screwdriver. The tip of the screwdriver has the capacity to fit the head of a Philips screw, and when it manifests this capacity it contributes to the overall functioning of the screwdriver. But it only does this given that other parts of the screwdriver also manifest capacities of their own, such as the shaft of the screwdriver maintaining its shape and physical integrity when turned (Koslicki 2018, 213). Note also that this dependence is generic; the tip of the screwdriver can manifest its capacities as long as it is combined with some other parts of the screwdriver that are of the right kind. Because this dependence is generic it can explain why many composites can survive changes in their parts (Koslicki 2018, 215) while also explaining why they cannot survive being disassembled.

Two points concerning Koslicki's approach are worth mentioning here. First, it allows for different entities to be unified to different degrees (Koslicki 2018, 191). This naturally suggests that in order for an entity to count as a substance, it must be unified to a sufficiently high degree. Second, Koslicki's approach seems compatible with substances having substantial parts. For instance, on this approach an organism counts as a substance only if at least some of its parts (e.g., its cells) interactionally depend upon in each other to a high enough degree. But this allows that each cell is itself also unified to the relevant degree (e.g., at least some of *its* parts interactionally depend upon each other to the requisite degree). Koslicki's specific version of Unity thus leaves open the possibility of rejecting Simplicity.

The approach taken by Koslicki restricts substantial composition by placing constraints on how the parts of a composite are arranged. A different way of restricting substantial composition is to argue that the parts must depend on or be *inseparable* from the substance itself (Inman 2018, 93). Inman develops this idea in terms of identity-dependence: the parts or components must depend for their identity on belonging to that specific substance (101–2). Each composite substance is therefore a *grounding whole*, composed entirely of 'parts whose existence and identity are defined in terms of the particular whole of which they are a part' (103).[42] In contrast, x is a *grounded whole* iff x has at least one proper part y such that x depends for its identity on y (or, more specifically, on having y as a proper part) (102). Examples of grounded wholes include heaps and mereological sums. This conception of unity provides a straightforward account of why such entities are not substances. It also entails Simplicity, given Inman's (2018, 98) view that a substance cannot depend for its identity on any other concrete entity.

One worry with this proposal is that plausible candidate substances such as molecules and multi-cellular organisms are not grounding wholes. Entities of these kinds seem to contain parts that do not depend for their identities on belonging to any specific molecule or organism. It may be that some of these entities are not grounded wholes either; for example, it is not obvious that every organism must have some proper part that helps to determine which organism it is. This suggests that in addition to grounded and grounding wholes we should consider the possibility of an intermediate class of composite entities. A member of this class would be a whole such that not all of its parts depend for their identities upon it, but that is not itself identity-dependent on any of its parts (Lowe 1998, 164–5). As the example of organisms suggests, at least some composite entities with a good claim to be substances seem to belong to this class. (It may well turn out that entities of this class, if there are any, would be emergent complex substances – see Section 5.2.)

Inman deals with such entities in a different way, by invoking what he terms *substantial holism*. On this view, an entity that becomes a component of a composite subject is either essentially altered so that it becomes identity-dependent on the whole to which it belongs, or it ceases to exist (Inman 2018, 104–6, 252). For instance, if an organism comes into existence when certain cells are arranged in a specific way, those cells might have been substances prior to their being arranged in this way. But once the organism exists and includes them as parts, they either lose their substance status, becoming identity-independent on

---

[42] Inman (2018, 71–3) uses the terminology of 'grounding', but the notion of grounding he uses when discussing substances is in effect identity-dependence.

the organism, or they cease to exist and are replaced by numerically distinct but qualitatively similar items that depend for their identities on the organism (see also Oderberg 2007, 70–1; Toner 2008, 289). Conversely, when a cell is removed from an organism then strictly speaking it ceases to exist, but the portion of matter or stuff that composed it remains intact (Inman 2018, 238).

In support of substantial holism, Inman appeals to the thought that composition is a *generative* operation, in that 'composite objects are *constructed* or *generated* from their parts' (105; this notion of generation is very similar to that discussed in Section 4). Suppose that w is a composite substance constructed by composition from a and b. Inman claims that 'were a and b to remain essentially unaltered after the generation of w, it is difficult to see how w could fail to be *what it is* in virtue of a and b, and thus derivative on its proper parts', that is, dependent for its identity on them (106). To avoid this conclusion, Inman suggests that we accept substantial holism.

This argument requires that for w to be generated or constructed by composition from a and b, it is necessary that w's identity (i.e., which specific entity it is) be determined by the identities of a and b. But this assumption is open to question. For instance, consider a complex artefact: it seems plausible that it is generated by composition from other entities (its parts), but its identity is not obviously determined by which specific parts it has (at least if it could have had parts other than those it actually has or will have).

There are a number of possible objections to substantial holism, many of which Inman discusses in detail (2018, 236–75). I shall outline a slightly different problem for this theory. On the face of it, certain parts of composite substances can exist outside of any such composite and can be transferred from one composite substance to another. For instance, it seems that a cell need not cease to exist on being removed from a multi-cellular organism; it can persist through this change, retaining its causal powers (though unable to manifest many of them when not part of a larger organism). If integrated into another organism, again the cells persists, and now many of its powers can manifest themselves as it contributes to the functioning of the whole organism.[43] Furthermore, at many moments in this process it seems that the cell itself can survive changes to its own parts (e.g., losing or gaining a molecule or atom). This counts against Inman's suggestion that on being removed from the organism the cell ceases to exist but the same portion of matter survives, at least if portions of matter are understood to be identity-dependent on their parts. It suggests that the cell continues to exist when not a proper part of any organism, and that it is not dependent for its identity on the specific parts it has. And a natural – though by no means

---

[43] It is worth noting that while the account I am sketching in this paragraph does not assume Koslicki's interactional dependence approach outlined earlier, it is compatible with it and can be developed by appeal to it.

obligatory – way of understanding this is that the cell itself is a substance and remains a substance throughout the process. While this objection to substantial holism is hardly decisive, it indicates some of the difficulties this theory faces.

A final point about Unity is that it is relevant to another proposed criterion of substancehood, one I shall not be able to discuss in detail but which is worth mentioning. This is the idea that a substance must be able to persist through changes in its intrinsic properties (for versions of this criterion, see Ayers 1991, 84–5; Lowe 1998, 136, 144; Simons 1998, 237–8; Wiggins 2016, 46; for criticisms of this proposed criterion, see Hoffman & Rosenkrantz 1994, 29–33; Hoffman 2011, 495–8). Proponents of this criterion almost always take substances to *endure* through time rather than *perduring* (persisting in virtue of having different temporal parts at different times). In the case of simple substances, it might be that no metaphysical account of their enduring can be offered. That is, the identity of such a substance across time would not consist in the obtaining of any other facts (Lowe 1998, 169–70). But in the case of a composite substance it seems that we can give a positive account of its identity across time in terms of the arrangement or structuring of its parts being preserved across time and through changes (Lowe 1998, 168; see also Shoemaker 1997, 288; Jaworski 2016, 94; Koslicki 2018, 215). So for instance, an organism can survive losing or changing some of its cells provided that at each point it is made up of cells arranged in such a way that the organism still has its essential features (e.g., it can metabolise certain chemicals). Exactly which changes an organism can live through will thus be at least partly to do with how its parts are arranged, and how its parts are arranged will be at least partly to do with what kind of entity it is.

In the preceding three sections I have outlined and discussed a number of different candidate criteria for substancehood: Independence, Ungroundedness, Ultimate Substance, Simplicity, and Unity. Some of these are necessary conditions on substances, others can be understood as proposed analyses of what it is to be a substance. It is an open question as to whether any of these criteria are successful, or to what degree (e.g., Ultimate Subject may be a necessary condition on substancehood but it plausibly falls short of a complete analysis). One other point to mention is that I have not considered ways in which these criteria could be combined. It may be that, for instance, a combination of Independence (say Identity Independence) and Unity will provide the best account of substancehood (see Gorman 2006).

6 Arguments for and against Substances

In this section, I shall turn to Q3, concerning arguments for and against the existence of substances. In practice, many such arguments will concern whether or not substances *must* (or must not) exist, or must exist (or not) given certain assumptions. It is also worth noting that many of the arguments to be considered are not framed specifically in terms of substance, but in terms of whether there are (or must be) entities satisfying some of the criteria outlined in Sections 3–5. Since some of these criteria were necessary rather than sufficient conditions for substancehood, many arguments supporting the existence of entities that satisfy some of these criteria would not, if successful, establish the existence of any substances. That said, these arguments are clearly relevant to the question of whether or not there are any substances.

6.1 Arguments in Favour of Substances

In Section 3.1, I mentioned a methodological distinction to do with whether or not one takes entities of specific kinds as paradigm substances. This distinction is relevant to arguments in support of the existence of substances. Suppose one takes certain entities to be paradigm substances. One will then face two questions:

(1) do such entities exist?
(2) do such entities count as substances (i.e., do they meet some or all of the criteria discussed in Sections 3–5)?

For instance, suppose one takes ordinary objects such as organisms or artefacts to count as substances. The default view is that there are entities of these kinds. Nevertheless, the existence of such entities, at least as they are usually understood, has been questioned. For instance, Van Inwagen (1990, 98–100) denies the existence of inanimate ordinary objects, assuming that they are composites. As regards (2), there are various positions that allow that ordinary objects exist but that would rule out their counting as fundamental entities (see Section 7.1). Two of the best-known of these positions are the *bundle theory* (on which each ordinary object is identified with a bundle of properties) and the *substratum theory* (on which each ordinary object is identified with a combination of properties and a bare substratum). Each of these positions entails that ordinary objects are constructed out of and dependent upon ontologically prior entities (i.e., properties and/or bare substrata); so plausibly, on neither of these views would ordinary objects count as substances as the category of substance is understood in this Element.

Each of these positions also faces well-known objections. For instance, it is often doubted whether there could be any such entity as a propertyless or bare substratum (see Section 5.1). Bundle theories that take properties to be universals face a well-known dilemma concerning the *Principle of the Identity of Indiscernibles*. Very roughly, this principle entails that numerically distinct entities cannot share all of their properties; the problem is that a bundle theory that takes properties to be universals seems to entail that such a scenario is indeed possible (for a summary of these and other arguments against bundle theories and substratum theories, see Loux 2006, 84–115). If these objections to bundle theories and substratum theories are successful they would provide indirect support for positing substances, since they would in effect rule out two of the main non-substance ontologies (though there are other non-substance ontologies – see Section 6.3).

It is also worth adding that questions (1) and (2) will apply in different ways to different candidate substances. In the case of ordinary objects, (2) is arguably a more difficult question to answer affirmatively than (1). In contrast, if one takes an entity such as God to be a paradigmatic substance, (1) would seem to be a more pressing matter than (2).

Suppose one adopts the second methodological approach, defining substances as entities that meet certain theoretical criteria (e.g., those discussed in Sections 3–5). In this case question (2) is less important. What are required are reasons to think that there are any entities that satisfy the stated criteria.[44] In the recent literature on substance, the most widely discussed criteria have been Independence and perhaps Ungroundedness. Therefore, in the rest of this subsection, I shall consider arguments for whether or not there are entities that are ungrounded or ontologically independent.

The view that there must be independent or ungrounded entities is *foundationalism* (this is a simplified gloss; see Bliss & Priest 2018, 2–10).[45] Perhaps the most familiar kind of argument in support of foundationalism is that fundamental entities are required to stop a *vicious regress* arising from the existence of dependent or grounded entities. For instance, Lowe (1998) suggests that there cannot be infinitely descending chains of entities standing in relations of identity-dependence with each other.[46] He adds that while he doubts this claim can be proven, he finds 'the vertiginous implication of its denial barely comprehensible' (158). Likewise, Schaffer (2010a, 62) writes that in a world without fundamental entities, 'being would be infinitely deferred, never achieved'.[47]

---

[44] Again, since some of these criteria were merely necessary conditions on substancehood, providing such reasons might not establish that there are substances.

[45] In addition, while I am glossing foundationalism in terms of entities that are independent or ungrounded, these are arguably different conceptions of foundationalism. For comparison, see Bennett 2017, 105–18; and Michael Raven's (2016) distinction between fundamentality and foundations.

[46] A chain of dependence is a collection of entities each member of which stands in a relation of dependence to at least one of the other members. Likewise, there can be chains of grounding.

[47] These claims are closely related to the roles of providing a foundation of being and explaining the other entities in the hierarchy of being (Section 2.2). In the literature it is common to see such claims discussed in terms of whether chains of dependence or grounding must be *well-founded* (see, e.g., Dixon 2016).

These claims express intuitions that many have shared. But it is not clear if they offer anything more than intuitive plausibility. To go beyond this, to show that these regresses really are *vicious*, requires showing that any view without ungrounded or independent entities leads to unacceptable conclusions. To simplify matters, let us work with grounding. There are two main alternatives to foundationalism regarding grounding (assuming one accepts that some entities are grounded). An *infinitist* world is one in which there can be infinitely descending grounding chains which fail to include an ungrounded member (Morganti 2018, 259). In a *coherentist* world, distinct entities could stand in circular grounding chains (262–3). Unlike infinitism, this requires altering some of the formal features of grounding assumed in Section 4.1 (e.g., allowing that grounding can be reflexive and symmetrical). Neither coherentism nor infinitism as characterised exclude ungrounded entities, but in what follows I shall be concerned with the possibility of coherentist and infinitist worlds containing no ungrounded entities.

Against coherentism one might argue that it involves an objectionable circularity, one that is closely connected to problems with circular explanations (Lowe 1998, 145). In response, Elizabeth Barnes (2018, 66) points out that the shortcomings of circular explanations are epistemic or pragmatic, and it is doubtful whether such shortcomings apply to grounding or to metaphysical explanation if either of these is understood as a worldly relation. Furthermore, Naomi Thompson (2018b) has offered examples of symmetrical explanations that are allowed for by certain theoretical approaches. For instance, on mathematical structuralism the nature of each mathematical object is explained in terms of the structure to which it belongs, and this object also helps explain the nature of every other object in that structure (118). Thompson further suggests that this example can be understood in terms of symmetrical grounding (118; see also 110–12 for further examples).

Turning to infinitism, one way to understand the vicious regress argument is as specifically targeting this position; it is precisely the prospect of infinitely descending identity-dependence that Lowe finds 'vertiginous'. But again, it is difficult to go beyond this intuition. One tempting option is to argue as follows: in a maximal grounding chain with no ungrounded entity, it may be that the existence of each member of the chain is explained by the members that ground it; but what has not been explained, and plausibly cannot be explained in this way, is the existence of the entire chain.

In assessing this worry we should distinguish between *mediate questions* (questions concerning each specific entity) and *global questions*, questions concerning all of the entities (Bliss 2013, 408). The infinitist can argue that the grounding chain is not posited to answer the global question of why the chain as a whole exists. Rather, it is intended to provide a model of how each of a series of grounded entities could exist without having to appeal to ungrounded entities (Bliss 2013, 408; for further criticism of regress arguments against infinitism, see Bliss & Priest 2018, 17–25).

A related objection to infinitism is briefly sketched by Inman (2018), who points out that positing ungrounded entities in principle allows for an explanation of why there are any grounded entities at all: 'It is one thing for there to be an explanation of each grounded entity in a domain, quite another for there to be an explanation for why the class of grounded entities exist in that domain in the first place' (61).[48] Infinitely descending chains of ground do not seem able to provide such an explanation, but a fundamental level of ungrounded entities seems well suited to do so.

In response to a similar suggestion, Ricki Bliss (2019, 365) points out that a class of entities is typically understood to be grounded in its members, so the question of why the class of grounded entities exists can be explained by appealing to each grounded entity. But I think Inman's point can be framed in a way that avoids this response. I glossed it earlier as the question of 'why there are any grounded entities at all'. This formulation should not be understood as asking why a specific class of entities exists.[49] It is better thought of in a different way: to be a grounded entity requires meeting a certain condition, and why does there exist any entity whatsoever that meets this condition? Stated in this way, the question cannot be answered by appealing to any of the grounded entities (unless, perhaps, grounding is allowed to be reflexive or symmetrical); but it can be answered by appeal to ungrounded entities.

It might be objected that this is a global question, and so is vulnerable to the response discussed earlier, that it is illegitimate to saddle the non-foundationalist with a task she did not set out to perform. But while it may be that infinitism is not motivated by answering this question, nonetheless the question seems legitimate. At any rate, if one thinks the question should not be posed or does not require an answer, one should offer reasons to support such claims.

6.2 Arguments That There Are No Substances

In this sub-section and the next, I shall consider various arguments against substances. In Section 6.3, I shall consider *indirect* arguments, specifically arguments for non-substance ontologies, which if successful would preclude

---

[48] Inman restricts the question he poses to why there are any ungrounded entities in a domain D. I am assuming that D includes every existing entity.

[49] Nor should it be understood as asking of any of the entities that exist why they happen to be grounded.

the need for positing substances. In this sub-section, I shall consider two *direct* arguments for the conclusion that there are no substances. The first direct argument is that given a certain view of how metaphysics should be carried out, the category of substance is of no use in trying to understand reality.[50] The second is an argument that there can be no entities that satisfy a central criterion of substancehood.

To introduce the first argument, consider a possible ontology hinted at by Tim Maudlin (2007, 86–101). Very roughly, Maudlin suggests that the ontology of fundamental posits of physics can be accounted for in terms of mathematical structures termed *fibre bundles*. This would seem to rule out substance ontologies of fundamental physical entities, but Maudlin also draws a broader lesson. The method of tying metaphysical claims to our best scientific theories suggests not only that there may be no substances; it suggests that substance is the wrong *kind* of category to yield any useful knowledge of reality. As he puts it,

> For example, modern electromagnetic theory holds that what we call the 'electromagnetic field' just *is* the connection on a fiber bundle. ... if one asks whether, in this picture, the electromagnetic field is a *substance* or an instance of a *universal* or a *trope*, or some combination of these, none of the options seems very useful. If the electromagnetic field is a connection on a fiber bundle, then one understands what it is by studying fiber bundles directly, not by trying to translate modern mathematics into archaic philosophical terminology. (101)

It may well be that Maudlin is right regarding the electromagnetic field. That said, in response to this specific example it is worth noting two things. First, the question of which ontology best fits our current understanding of fundamental physics is a matter of ongoing debate (see Sections 7.2 and 7.3). Second, even if there are no substances at the level described by fundamental microphysics, this does not by itself preclude substances existing in the physical world. For example, it might be that certain ordinary objects will turn out to be identity-independent or not fully metaphysically explainable by even a completed physics (see Sections 5.2 and 5.3). Such entities would at least be promising candidates to count as substances, even if no substances featured in the world as characterised by physics.

---

[50] A related argument against substances appeals to parsimony: the idea being that the category of substance is redundant since it is not needed to characterise reality or explain any phenomena, and so should be dispensed with on grounds of theoretical economy. In practice such an argument will be part of a package along with a defence of some other ontological system, the idea being that substances are not needed because we can get by with, for example, tropes, events, or some combination of other categories. Therefore, the argument from parsimony is better thought of as part of the indirect arguments to be considered in Section 6.3.

Maudlin considers a way of developing the first of these points: 'Given the dependence of so much of the fiber-bundle structure on objects inhabiting a single connected space-time, one might be inclined to go Spinozistic: there is but one substance, and it is the whole of connected space-time' (102; see also Section 7.3 of this Element). However, he dismisses this suggestion as largely useless: 'if there is only *one* substance and every physical fact corresponds to a distinct property of *it*, then we are getting no structural insight at all into the nature of the world by being informed of which substances exist' (102). But whether this dismissal is warranted surely depends on what is meant by 'structural insight'. It is certainly true that this Spinozistic view does not reveal much about the *physical* structure of reality, in the sense of a structure that might be accessible by means of physics. But if correct it would surely carry important information about reality's *metaphysical* structure. For instance, it would entail that space-time is not reducible to a collection of space-time points, and that it is not constituted by relations among spatiotemporal entities. These entailments would cut down the range of possible ways the world might turn out to be, metaphysically speaking, which is one way of thinking of them as metaphysically informative.

Maudlin's skepticism about the category of substance is rooted in a more general meta-metaphysical approach. Roughly speaking, he is skeptical of metaphysical claims that go beyond reasonably plausible scientific theories (184–91). This kind of skepticism is characteristic of a *naturalistic* methodology in metaphysics, one that is trenchantly stated in the first chapter of Ladyman and Ross's (2007) book. If one adopts this methodology, one may well doubt whether the notion of 'substance' as it is understood in this Element draws any useful distinctions or even has any genuine content. Hence the first argument against substance stated at the beginning of this sub-section: on a certain view of how metaphysics should be carried out, the category of substance is of no use in trying to understand reality.

A proper discussion of the methodology of metaphysics is beyond the scope of this Element. Nevertheless, it is worth noting that there are methodological approaches that either explicitly allow for substances or at least seem to make room for this category. Some of these alternatives are themselves presented as versions of naturalistic metaphysics (e.g., Morganti & Tahko 2017). It is also worth noting that the demarcation between the kind of strongly naturalistic metaphysics favoured by Maudlin and methods that are less tightly tied to scientific theorising can itself be questioned. At any rate, it is not clear how sharply this demarcation can be drawn, or whether there are clear reasons to favour one approach over the others (McKenzie 2021).

To be clear: the existence of such methodological debates is not by itself reason to accept the usefulness or applicability of the concept 'substance'. And it is reasonable to ask substance theorists to say more about their methods, for example, with regard to modal epistemology (see Mallozzi et al. 2021). But it is also reasonable for substance theorists to discuss first-order matters (e.g., Q1–Q4) without having first resolved these methodological issues. As to whether the category of substance is a useful one, to a large extent this matter can be settled only by considering specific substance ontologies and how they can contribute to our understanding (e.g., with regard to the roles described in Section 2.2). These remarks by no means constitute a full-throated defence of the category of substance, but they indicate some lines of response to the first argument against it.

The second direct argument I shall consider is an a priori argument for the conclusion that there can be no such entities as substances. Interestingly, this argument is proposed by Schaffer, who I have previously cited as one of the main recent proponents of substance. In setting out this argument, Schaffer (2013) introduces substances as fundamental entities, where an entity is fundamental if it does not depend on anything else (68). He suggests that while entities necessarily belong to their categories, fundamentality is not a necessary feature of any entity. In support of this claim Schaffer cites examples of candidate substances that, he claims, could fail to be fundamental: it might be possible for a particular electron to be divisible and so dependent on its parts; a particular self might be funda-mental in a dualist world but not fundamental in a physicalist world;[51] and the entire cosmos might be embedded in a larger whole, in which case it would not be a substance as far as Schaffer himself is concerned (81).[52] If no entities are necessarily fundamental, then no entities count as substances on Schaffer's conception of the latter.

I shall raise three issues with this argument. The first issue is that it is not obvious that it applies to *every* candidate substance. For instance, if God exists, could He have failed to be fundamental (a tricky test of divine omnipotence)? Or perhaps one could appeal to necessarily indivisible particles. If there were such entities, then it would not be possible for them to fail to be fundamental by depending on their parts.

A second issue is that Schaffer's discussion of the examples he does consider is open to question. For instance, it is not obvious that the very same self could

---

[51] Schaffer puts this point in terms of a mind, but I think that a self (or subject of experiences) is a better candidate to be a substance (see Section 7.4).

[52] On the first and last of these examples, see Sections 7.2 and 7.3 respectively.

exist in a physicalist world and also in a dualist world.[53] A typical gloss on physicalism is that it entails that there is nothing over and above the physical entities (Dowell 2006, 1; Melnyk 2008, 1281). Let us suppose that in a dualist world a self is something over and above any physical entity. It is at least not obvious that the very same entity could be something over and above any physical entities in one possible world and be nothing over and above some physical entities in another possible world (compare with Levine & Trogdon 2009, 356–61).

A third issue with Schaffer's argument is that it is not obvious that for all forms of ontological dependence, an entity that is not dependent could have been dependent. Consider first rigid existential dependence: necessarily, if x exists then y exists. This entails that there is no possible world in which x exists and y does not. Now suppose that it is contingent that x rigidly depends on y. In that case, there is a possible world in which x exists and y does not. But this contradicts the formulation of rigid existential dependence. Therefore, if x rigidly existentially depends on y it does so necessarily; it is not possible that x could be (or could have been) existentially independent of y.[54]

Now consider the opposite claim: if x does *not* rigidly existentially depend on y, could x be (or have been) rigidly existentially dependent on y? That is, is x's existential independence with respect to y merely contingent? It is difficult to see how this is possible. If x is *not* rigidly existentially dependent upon y, then there is some possible world at which x exists and y does not. But were x rigidly dependent upon y, there could be no such world. Again, the first of these conditions seems to rule out the second.

The same point seems to hold with regard to essential dependence: if it is essential to x that p (i.e., if it is part of what x is that p holds), it just seems impossible for x, that very entity, to be such that x could exist even if p failed to hold. Conversely, if it is *not* essential to x that p (i.e., if it is *not* part of what x is that p), then this seems to rule out that it could be, or could have been, essential to x that p. What is essential to an entity is definitive of what that very entity (or kind of entity) is. The very same (kind of) entity could not have a different real definition in different possible worlds. Therefore, if x is essentially independent of p, this does not seem to be a contingent fact.

It is worth also considering how the third issue with Schaffer's argument applies given Schaffer's own framework. Schaffer (2009a, 373) defines

---

[53] Schaffer (2013, 81) would prefer to put this in terms of counterparts: the question is whether a self in a dualist world could have a counterpart in a physicalist world. I prefer to treat individuals as capable of existing in different possible worlds, but I think the points I shall raise would also be valid if made in terms of counterparts.

[54] Thanks to Claudio Calosi for helping to formulate this argument.

fundamental entities as ungrounded. In this framework, the question is whether an entity that in the actual world has no grounds could have grounds in some other world (in other words, whether an entity that in fact satisfies UC does so only contingently). It seems to me that Schaffer's own view of grounding does not entail a straightforward answer to this question. Schaffer himself clearly thinks that an entity that satisfies UC can do so only contingently, but his argument for this involves appealing to examples that I have already suggested are not conclusive. On the other hand, if an entity that is in fact ungrounded could have grounds, this strongly suggests that an entity that is in fact grounded could exist without having any grounds at all. This suggestion sounds counter-intuitive to me, but it is not clear whether anything more than intuition can be marshaled against it (see also Section 4.1 regarding the relation between grounding and ontological dependence).

This discussion indicates a limitation of the third issue I raised for Schaffer's argument; there is a conception of fundamentality (as ungroundedness) with which his argument *may* be compatible. But conversely, the third issue indicates a limitation on Schaffer's argument. At best, this argument works only given certain views of fundamentality, for example, as ungroundedness (and thus only for certain conceptions of substance).

6.3 Alternatives to Substance Ontologies

Even if direct arguments against substances do not work, we may still have reason to forego entities belonging to this category. The most straightforward reason would be to defend an ontology that does not require us to posit substances. I shall briefly outline some of these alternative, non-substance ontologies, and then examine one in more detail.[55]

Alternatives to substance ontologies can be grouped into two camps. The first camp includes what are sometimes referred to as *thing ontologies*, ontologies that posit discrete entities (Esfeld 2021, 459). Substance ontologies are themselves thing ontologies, and a substance ontologist can posit fundamental entities other than substances. A thing ontology is an alternative to substance ontologies if it does not include substances. One such alternative would be a *trope ontology* (Campbell 1990). Tropes are particularised properties (e.g., the particular redness or roundness of a specific ball). In a trope ontology, tropes are fundamental, and typically other entities are analysed in terms of tropes (so, for

---

[55] Coherentism and infinitism are alternatives to substance ontologies insofar as they allow for there to be no ungrounded or independent entities. It is worth noting that while some of the alternative ontologies I shall discuss are compatible with coherentism and infinitism, some (perhaps all) are also compatible with foundationalism.

instance, the red ball would be analysed as a bundle of co-present tropes).[56] Another alternative posits *universal properties* such as redness or roundness as the fundamental entities (O'Leary-Hawthorne & Cover 1998). Such properties, unlike tropes, can be shared by multiple entities. Again, proponents of such an ontology will typically seek to analyse other entities in terms of universal properties (e.g., the ball would be analysed as a bundle of co-instantiated properties). Yet another alternative posits *processes* as fundamental entities. There are a number of ways of characterising processes. For instance, Helen Steward (2012) suggests that processes can themselves undergo changes and do not have their temporal parts essentially: as she puts it, they are 'mereologically and modally robust' (383). In these respects they are like substances, but unlike substances processes are themselves *changings*, 'bringings about of results by things or collections of things' (383). Again, the process ontologist can suggest that other entities can be analysed in terms of processes. Steward herself does not advocate this programme. Johanna Seibt (2009) does, though her notion of process is in some respects rather different to Steward's.

The second camp of alternative ontologies includes *non-thing ontologies*, mainly *stuff ontologies* (Esfeld 2021, 464). In this context, 'stuff' means something like continuous matter as opposed to any plurality of discrete entities. A stuff ontology that is an alternative to a substance ontology would be one with one or more kinds of stuff but no substances made out of stuff (Van Inwagen 1993, 27). Against this kind of stuff ontology Van Inwagen argues that it is inconsistent with current physics, which suggests that everything is made out of electrons and quarks that are not themselves made out of anything else and seem to be discrete entities themselves (27–8; see also Maudlin 2007, 185; and Section 7.2 of this Element).

I shall not be able to consider arguments for and against each of these alternative ontologies, but in the remainder of this sub-section, I shall examine a specific alternative ontology in more detail. Daniel Nolan (2011, 285–7) argues that ordinary objects such as artefacts and animals are *events* of specific kinds.[57] Nolan prefers (though is not committed to) a relatively fine-grained conception of events; distinct events can occur at the same time and place and involve the same objects (288). Nolan's view is plausibly understood as a non-substance ontology; at least it is compatible with there being no substances.

---

[56] Alternatively a trope ontologist can hold that there are no other entities save tropes. A similar point can be made for the other alternative ontologies I shall consider presently.

[57] Nolan refers to such ordinary objects as 'things'. I am using the term 'thing' in a somewhat different way, to describe the group of 'thing' ontologies of which Nolan's event ontology is one. Therefore, I shall use the term 'objects' to refer to what Nolan terms 'things'.

Nolan offers a number of different arguments to support this view. One is an *argument from parsimony regarding necessary connections*. The thought is that we can explain relations between a specific event and the object that undergoes it (e.g., between myself and the event of my sitting down) by understanding this as a relation between two distinct events that necessarily overlap (e.g., this short event and my life history). This has the advantage of reducing two problems (necessary connections between distinct events, and necessary connections between events and the objects that undergo them) to one (292). But while this approach might reduce the *number* of problems, it seems to deepen the problem left over. The necessary connection between the event of my sitting down and myself runs from the event to me; it is necessary for this particular event that it happens to me, and it is plausibly not necessary for me to undergo this particular event (more on this presently). But it is not at all obvious that we should say the same thing about this short event and the longer event (my life history) with which it overlaps. Plausibly, this shorter event could have occurred without my entire life history having unfolded as it had up to that point.

Nolan also outlines an *argument from borderline cases*, entities such as forest fires and storms. Each of these, he suggests, can be described in ways that make them seem like events (e.g., they start and finish) and also in ways that make them seem like objects – fires 'can move from place to place, they can grow or shrink, they take up space' (294). Nolan suggests that these borderline cases support the thought that the distinction between events and objects is not a genuine ontological difference but a matter of how it suits us to classify different entities (294).

However, other approaches to borderline cases are available, which are compatible with holding that there is an ontological distinction between events and objects. It may be possible to account for the existence of borderline ontological cases (entities that do not fall clearly into either of two distinct categories) in terms of our lack of understanding of the nature of these entities, in a manner similar to an epistemicist response to problems of vagueness (Williamson 1994). Another strategy would be to suggest that these cases, far from showing that the distinction between objects and events should be collapsed, suggest the need for further categories of entity, for example, entities that are similar to paradigmatic events in some respects but importantly different from them in others (ditto for paradigmatic objects). Either way, there seem to be ways of addressing borderline cases without concluding that there is no distinction between substances and other entities, or that the category of 'substance' should be subsumed into that of 'event'.

Finally, Nolan (2011) addresses the objection that ordinary objects cannot be events because objects and events have different modal profiles. For instance, I could have had a different life history, so I cannot be identical with my actual life history (297). Nolan offers two responses to this objection. The first is that de re modal predications are *inconstant*; roughly, the truth of different de re modal claims depends on how the entity in question is described. This in principle allows us to explain why objects and events have different modal profiles, even though each object is identical with a certain event: 'talked about as a history, an entity has one modal profile associated with it, talked about as a thing, another' (297). I shall not be able to discuss this approach to de re modal predications, but it is worth noting that it remains controversial (e.g., Fine 2003; Mackie 2021).

Nolan's (2011) second response is to distinguish events of *different grain* (e.g., the event of my talking as opposed to the event of my talking loudly). Nolan suggests that these events will have different modal profiles; specifically, coarser-grained events will be more modally flexible (i.e., able to occur in a wider range of possible worlds). He then suggests that 'there are plausibly events with the right modal profile to match things', and it is with these events that objects should be identified (299).

One problem with this response is that Nolan does not provide an onto-logical account of events. So it is not clear why one should accept that there is a single ontological category that includes both entities with very fine-grained modal profiles and entities with modal profiles as coarse-grained as those of tables or cats. One might also wonder if the argument could not be run the other way: perhaps the category 'objects' might turn out to accommodate not only relatively coarse-grained entities such as myself, but such fine-grained and modally fragile specimens as my slowly sitting down? If this proposal sounds like a linguistic trick, then likewise, I suggest, we should be suspicious of Nolan's.

To some extent the arguments for and against Nolan's preferred ontology can be generalised. In particular, a number of alternative ontologies face modal objections of the same kind as discussed earlier. For instance, bundle theories face problems as to how an entity that is identical with a bundle of properties could have been made of properties other than those that actually compose it (Van Cleve 1985). In contrast, substances are standardly understood as being capable of having existed with many properties other than those they actually have (see Section 2.2). Therefore, a conception of ordinary objects as sub-stances does not face this modal problem, and to that extent has an advantage over many of the alternative ontologies.

7 Candidate Substances

Finally we turn to Q4. In this section, I shall consider four different types of candidate substances. Any proposed answer to this question will face the two further questions outlined in Section 6.1:

(1) do such entities exist?
(2) do such entities count as substances?

It is also worth noting that candidate substances might be advanced as *exclusive* candidates (as being the only substances), or as one kind of candidate among others.

7.1 Ordinary Objects

The first type of candidate substances are what I have termed *ordinary objects*, where this class is understood as including many objects we perceive and interact with on a daily basis, such as organisms, material bodies, and perhaps artefacts. This type of candidate can also be thought to include a range of entities that feature in well-established scientific theories, such as cells, molecules, and planets (though not fundamental particles or the entire cosmos – see Sections 7.2 and 7.3). As should be clear, the term 'ordinary objects' applies to entities of many different kinds, and there is room for disagreement concerning which of these kinds provide suitable candidates and which do not.

As regards (1), the default position is that many ordinary objects exist, though there is debate on this score (see Van Inwagen 1990, 98–100). The main issue facing this first group of candidates is (2), whether ordinary objects count as substances. One familiar kind of challenge to the substancehood of ordinary objects is that they are *ontologically reducible* to the entities that compose them, in roughly the following sense: what it is for an ordinary object to exist and have the intrinsic properties it has is for its components to exist, have certain properties, and be arranged in certain ways. It seems clear that an object that is reducible in this way is not a substance on most of the independence or ungroundedness criteria outlined earlier. It is possible that such an object could be both highly unified and an ultimate subject, but it is doubtful whether Unity or Ultimate Subject, either alone or together, could be sufficient for substancehood.

This reductionist challenge comes in two main forms. One seeks to show that ordinary objects are reducible to their physical, chemical, or biological parts (e.g., molecules are reducible to atoms arranged in certain ways).[58]

---

[58] Perhaps some ordinary objects are reducible to such parts in certain contexts. For instance, the reduction base for artefacts might include the socio-cultural contexts in which they are made or used.

This approach would not work if ordinary objects were strongly emergent (Section 5.2), and plausibly it would not work either if the identities of ordinary objects were not determined by any of their parts (Section 5.3). The other form the reductionist challenge can take is to reduce ordinary objects either to their properties or to combinations of properties and a substratum (for discussion see Loux 2006, 107–17).

Ordinary objects face other challenges to their substancehood. One challenge appeals to the thought that many ordinary objects (e.g., organisms or geographical features) have vague or indeterminate boundaries (Simons 1998, 249). The thought here is that such entities do not count as individuals (in the sense of there being determinate facts of the matter as to which entities they are), or perhaps lack the requisite level of unity to count as substances. Lowe has responded to this line of thought by urging that we should think differently about these cases. While it may be indeterminate which group of entities help to *compose* an ordinary complex object, it does not follow that the identity of that object is itself indeterminate, at least if the identity of the ordinary object is not determined by the identity of its parts (Lowe 2012, 105–10; see also Inman 2018, 190–4).

A related challenge is offered by Howard Robinson (2016). Consider a physical entity such as a molecule, which came into existence at a certain time and is formed out of certain material (i.e., specific atoms). We can ask whether that very molecule could have come into existence at a different time or been fashioned from different material. And for certain counterfactual scenarios of this kind, there will be no determinate fact of the matter as to whether or not that very entity exists (195). Therefore, Robinson suggests, this molecule cannot be a 'full-fledged' individual, one for which there is a fact of the matter as to whether or not it exists in any specified counterfactual situation (194). If one assumes that substances are individuals, Robinson's argument would eliminate most ordinary objects (along with all other physical candidate substances).

One possible reply to this argument is that it does not clearly work against simple substances. Lowe (1998, 170) argues that the identity of such substances across time is primitive; it does not consist in the obtaining of any other facts. It seems possible to go further and make the same claim regarding their identity in counterfactual situations: that is, a simple substance's existing in a certain counterfactual scenario does not consist in the obtaining of any other facts. If this is correct, then Robinson's argument could be blocked for such substances. For each counterfactual scenario, there might be a determinate fact of the matter as to whether or not x exists in that scenario, even though we may not be able to distinguish between those scenarios that would include x and those scenarios that would not.

Robinson's challenge can also be contested even in the case of composite substances. Such substances will have criteria of identity. A criterion of identity for a composite substance x and a composite substance y is a principle that states that x is identical with y iff certain relations hold between other entities (e.g., the parts of x and the parts of y). But this does not entail that *which* entity of its kind x is (i.e., its individual identity) is determined by *which* entities are its parts (Lowe 1998, 168–9).[59] Therefore, a composite substance need not depend for its individual identity on the parts from which it was originally made, and arguably it need not depend for its individual identity on the specific time at which it began to exist. And this at least leaves open the possibility that such substances have primitive counterfactual identities; that for each counterfactual scenario there might be a primitive fact of the matter as to whether or not x exists in that scenario.[60]

In addition to considering ordinary objects in general, it is possible to challenge the substancehood of certain kinds of ordinary object. For instance, it has been argued that organisms are best thought of as processes rather than substances. For criticisms of these arguments, see the articles by Steward (2020) and Morgan (in press).

7.2 Simple Particles

The second type of candidate substances I shall consider are *simple particles*, particles with no substantial parts. One way to develop this proposal is to appeal to the particles postulated in the current Standard Model of physics; alternatively, one might appeal to particles that would be posited in a hypothetical completed physics. If there are such particles, they would satisfy Simplicity and plausibly at least some versions of Independence. They would seem to be ultimate subjects, and it is natural to think that the existence of such entities could not be metaphysically explained. Thus, if there are any simple particles, at first glance they would be excellent candidate substances.

Furthermore, if there are such particles it is very tempting to think that they are the *only* substances (Heil (2012, 41) considers this an open possibility). One way to develop this idea is what Jaegwon Kim (1998) terms 'the familiar

---

[59] Criteria of identity are informative principles concerning the relation of identity. This is different to the individuality of a specific substance, there being a fact as to which entity it is (on the distinction between individuality and the relation of identity, see Section 3.5).

[60] It is worth noting that these responses to Robinson's argument come at a steep epistemic price: in effect, they would render the identities of many substances inscrutable in many counterfactual scenarios.

multilayered model that views the world as stratified into different "levels" . . . organized in a hierarchical structure':

> The bottom level is usually thought to consist of elementary particles, or whatever our best physics is going to tell us are the basic bits of matter out of which all material things are composed. As we go up the ladder, we successively encounter atoms, molecules, cells, larger living organisms, and so on. The ordering relation that generates the hierarchical structure is the mereological (part-whole) relation: entities belonging to a given level, except those at the very bottom, have an exhaustive decomposition, without remainder, into entities belonging to the lower levels (15).

This model is usually understood as entailing that only the elementary particles are absolutely fundamental, and so only they would be strong candidate substances. Another way to develop the idea that simple particles are the only substances is *compositional nihilism*: all that exists are simple particles, which never compose any complex entities (Van Inwagen 1990, 72).

Regarding question (1), it is debatable whether there are any simple particles. While the Standard Model does postulate a range of particles, it is not clear that any of them are simple (in the sense of not being composed of further particles). Schaffer (2003, 501) argues that there are reasons to take seriously the possibility that our world is *gunky*, that is, every concrete entity has a proper part. He also suggests that based on the history of theories in physics we should not assume that future microphysics will postulate fundamental simple particles (503–5).

Supposing for the sake of argument that there are fundamental simple physical particles, the next issue is whether they really are strong candidates to be substances (i.e., question (2)). It is sometimes thought that fundamental physical particles, especially when considered in the context of quantum mechanics, are not individuals, that is, there is no fact of the matter as to which particle of a specific kind is which (Simons 1998, 247–8; on the relevant notion of individuals as opposed to non-individuals, see Section 3.5 of this Element). This would arguably rule out such particles as candidate substances. Alternatively, it might be thought that quantum mechanics underdetermines whether or not particles are individuals (Ladyman & Ross 2007, 135–7). This would not by itself rule out particles being substances, but it has been thought to pave the way for relational or structuralist conceptions of particles, which are typically contrasted with the idea of substances as identity-independent (138–40). But there are also metaphysical interpretations of quantum mechanics on which particles are individuals. For instance, one might think that the individuality of quantum particles is *primitive*, that is, irreducible to any of their other features (Dorato & Morganti 2013; for an overview of these and other options, see French 2019).

A second objection is that it is not clear if fundamental particles are substances or whether they should be understood as belonging to what seem to be alternative ontological categories, such as events, tropes, or fields. Indeed, the point can be pushed further: it is not clear in what sense many theories in fundamental physics, such as string theories and loop quantum gravity, posit particles at all (for an overview of the different ontologies suggested by fundamental physical theories, see Morganti 2020, 5–6).

7.3 Space-Time

A third type of candidate substances are space-time regions. A couple of distinctions are needed to clarify this suggestion. The first concerns *which* space-time regions might count as substances. On one view, many different regions or points are substances; on another, the whole of space-time is itself a single substance (Schaffer 2009b, 132). A second distinction concerns the relation between space-time regions and the entities that occupy them. On one view, *super-substantivalism*, space-time regions are the only spatio-temporal substances; on a rival view, space-time regions are substances and at least some of the entities occupying them are distinct substances (Schaffer 2009b, 133).[61] Super-substantivalism has obvious advantages in terms of ontological parsimony: rather than positing both space-time and some of its occupants as distinct kinds of substances, it makes do with just one kind (for further arguments, see Schaffer 2009b, 137–44). Against it, there is the worry that space-time regions have very different modal properties to many of the entities that occupy them. For instance, had I chosen a different career I would plausibly have occupied a different region of space-time to the one I actually occupy, but it is not possible for the space-time region I actually occupy to itself be located elsewhere in space-time. Schaffer (2009b, 145) responds to this by invoking a counterpart-theoretic account of de re modal truths (see also the discussion of inconstancy in Section 6.3).

As regards the first distinction, arguments that the whole of space-time is itself a substance are closely related to arguments that sub-regions or space-time points are not. For instance, Richard Healey (1995, 303) appeals to the idea that 'it is its place in a certain relational structure that makes p the spacetime point that it is'. That is, any space-time point, and plausibly any sub-region of space-time, depends for its identity on its specific place in an overall structure of other space-time points and regions (see also Schaffer 2009b, 135–6). In contrast, space-time as a whole does not belong to any larger spatio-temporal structure.

---

[61] There are different versions of super-substantivalism. In what follows, I shall focus on what Schaffer (2009b, 133) terms the 'identity view', which identifies material objects with the space-time regions they occupy.

Furthermore, Healey suggests that space-time is not dependent on the specific points or regions that it actually includes, and could have been made up of different parts (298). This suggests that space-time as a whole is ontologically prior to the points or regions it includes, and is thus a stronger candidate substance than them.

The whole of space-time's being a substance is compatible with many of the entities that occupy it also being substances. However, if the identity view of super-substantivalism is correct, each of these entities is identical with the space-time region it occupies. Given this, and given that the whole of space-time is ontologically prior to its sub-regions, it follows that space-time is also prior to any of the entities occupying its sub-regions. This line of thought suggests *priority monism*, the view that the whole concrete universe or cosmos is ontologically prior to all other concrete entities (Schaffer 2009b, 136). Strictly speaking, priority monism so defined does not entail that the cosmos is a fundamental entity on Schaffer's view, since it does not entail that there is nothing grounding the cosmos (344). However, in what follows I shall take priority monism to be the claim that the cosmos is a substance (see Heil 2012, 41, where this view is presented as a live option).

As regards question (1) concerning the existence of the cosmos, the priority monist can appeal to classical mereology, in particular the Axiom of Unrestricted Composition which 'guarantees the existence of the cosmos as the fusion of all actual concrete objects' (Schaffer 2010a, 34). Those of us wary of unrestricted composition will not find this very convincing (we may prefer to regard the cosmos as the maximal plurality of concrete entities rather than itself being a single entity). More significantly, this argument threatens to undermine the cosmos's claim to being a substance. If the cosmos is identical with the sum of all actual concrete objects, then the most natural way to think about it is as dependent for its existence and its identity on its proper parts (Lowe 2012, 93; Inman 2018, 242).

A second response to (1) is to appeal to the fact that the cosmos is the object of scientific (specifically cosmological) study (Schaffer 2010a, 34). For discussion of this response, see the works by Lowe (2012, 93), Jonathan Tallant (2015, 3105–6), and Inman (2018, 243).

The next issue is question (2), whether the cosmos counts as a substance. In addition to the argument from super-substantivalism just outlined, Schaffer presents a battery of other arguments in support of priority monism (for a summary, see Schaffer 2018). I shall briefly mention one of these. In an entangled system in quantum mechanics, the properties of the whole system do not supervene on the properties of its parts, but the properties of the parts supervene on properties of the system. Schaffer (2010a) suggests that entangled systems should thus be understood as more fundamental than their parts.

He then argues that the cosmos is a single entangled system, and therefore is more fundamental than any other concrete entity (51–5). Against this argument, it has been claimed that quantum entanglement can be understood not in terms of properties of the whole system, but in terms of fundamental entanglement relations holding between the entangled particles (Morganti 2009, 276–8; see also Calosi 2018).

A negative answer to (2) might be supported by theories in physics that suggest that space-time is derivative upon more fundamental, non-spatiotemporal structures (Wüthrich 2019). If any of these theories are correct then this would threaten the claim that space-time is a substance (though, as just noted, this might be compatible with the weaker version of priority monism defended by Schaffer). One possible response would be to modify priority monism: perhaps there will be a single fundamental entity but it will turn out to be something other than space-time (e.g., the wave function). An alternative response would be to accept that space-time emerges from non-spatiotemporal entities, but to deny that this rules it out as a substance. To defend this response would require characterising space-time as strongly ontologically emergent (see Section 5.2; contrast with Wüthrich 2019, 318).

7.4 The Self

The final type of candidate substances I shall consider are *selves*. I understand these to be *subjects of experience*, entities that have or can have conscious experiences. A more contentious claim is that selves can or must be rational agents or have intrinsic moral value. This would make selves close to *persons* as they are often discussed in the literature.

The most familiar way to think of selves as substances is *substance dualism*, roughly the view that a self is a substance distinct from any material or physical substance. Some recent discussions of what is framed as 'substance dualism' do not treat the self as a substance as I understand this notion, but characterise it as a bundle of properties or as composed of properties and a substratum (Schneider 2012; Yang 2015). Recent defences of what are recognisably versions of substance dualism in my preferred sense include the works by Foster (1991), Lowe (1996), Swinburne (2013), and various contributions in Loose and colleagues' (2018) volume.

It is also possible to defend *substance monism* regarding the self. For instance, *animalists* identify at least some selves (e.g., humans) with organisms (Snowdon 2014). As suggested in Section 7.1, organisms are often regarded as strong candidate substances, so it is at least open to the animalist to classify some selves as substances. Alternatively, a conception of selves as immaterial substances is compatible with denying that there are any material substances (Robinson 2016, 233).

As regards (1), concerning the existence of selves, some theorists are explicitly eliminativist. For instance, Thomas Metzinger (2003) supports this view by appealing to neuroscience, and Miri Albahari (2006) draws on Buddhist traditions. But eliminativist views about the self are very much in the minority.

There is much more discussion concerning whether or not selves are substances (i.e., question (2)). Proponents of the claim that the self is a substance have offered various arguments against reductive views (e.g., the bundle and substratum views mentioned earlier). John Foster (1991, 212–19) argues that our basic conception of token experiences is as occurring for and dependent upon selves in a way that rules out a self being partially or wholly composed of its own experiences. Lowe (1996, 25–32) argues that the identity of each individual experience is partly determined by the identity of the self that has it, and therefore the identity of a self is independent of the identities of its experiences. Robinson (2016, 235–42) argues that facts about the identity of selves (for instance in counter-factual situations), unlike facts about the identity of material entities, are not vague or determined by convention. Therefore selves are individuals: there are robust facts about which entity of its kind each self is, facts which, for instance, a bundle conception of the self cannot capture. Whether any of these arguments establishes that selves are substances is open to question; for critical discussion, see the contributions of Dainton (2008, 341–54), John Spackman (2013, 1057–8), and José Luis Bermúdez (2015).

References

Albahari, Miri (2006) *Analytical Buddhism: The Two-Tiered Illusion of Self.* Basingstoke: Palgrave Macmillan.

Anscombe, G. E. M. (1964) 'Substance', *Aristotelian Society Supplementary Volume* 38 (1): 69–78.

Aristotle (1984a [1963]) 'Categories' (trans. John L. Ackrill), in *The Complete Works of Aristotle: The Revised Oxford Translation* (ed. Jonathan Barnes). Princeton: Princeton University Press, 3–24.

Aristotle (1984b [1924]) 'Metaphysics' (trans. William D. Ross), in *The Complete Works of Aristotle: The Revised Oxford Translation* (ed. Jonathan Barnes). Princeton: Princeton University Press, 1552–728.

Armstrong, David M. (1997) *A World of States of Affairs*. Cambridge: Cambridge University Press.

Audi, Paul (2012) 'Grounding: Toward a Theory of the *In-Virtue-Of* Relation', *Journal of Philosophy* 109 (12): 685–711. http://doi.org/10.5840/jphil20121091232.

Ayers, Michael (1991) 'Substance: Prolegomena to a Realist Theory of Identity', *Journal of Philosophy* 88 (2): 69–90.

Barnes, Elizabeth (2018) 'Symmetric Dependence', in Ricki Bliss & Graham Priest (eds.), *Reality and Its Structure: Essays in Fundamentality*. Oxford: Oxford University Press, 50–69.

Bennett, Karen (2017) *Making Things Up*. Oxford: Oxford University Press.

Benovsky, Jiri (2016) *Meta-Metaphysics: On Metaphysical Equivalence, Primitiveness, and Theory Choice*. Cham: Springer.

Bermúdez, José Luis (2015) 'Selves, Bodies, and Self-Reference: Reflections on Jonathan Lowe's Non-Cartesian Dualism', *Journal of Consciousness Studies* 22 (11–12): 20–42.

Bliss, Ricki (2013) 'Viciousness and the Structure of Reality', *Philosophical Studies* 166 (2): 399–418. http://doi:10.1007/s11098-012-0043-0.

Bliss, Ricki (2019) 'What Work the Fundamental?', *Erkenntnis* 84 (2): 359–79. http://doi.org/10.1007/s10670-017-9962-7.

Bliss, Ricki & Priest, Graham (2018) 'The Geography of Fundamentality: An Overview', in Ricki Bliss & Graham Priest (eds.), *Reality and Its Structure: Essays in Fundamentality*. Oxford: Oxford University Press, 1–33.

Brenner, Andrew, Maurin, Anna-Sofia, Skiles, Alexander, Stenwall, Robin & Thompson, Naomi (2021) 'Metaphysical Explanation', in Edward N. Zalta (ed.), *The Stanford Encyclopedia of Philosophy.* https://plato.stanford.edu/archives/win2021/entries/metaphysical-explanation.

Broackes, Justin (2006) 'Substance', *Proceedings of the Aristotelian Society* 106 (1): 133–68.

Calosi, Claudio (2018) 'Quantum Monism: An Assessment', *Philosophical Studies* 175 (12): 3217–36. https://doi.org/10.1007/s11098-017-1002-6.

Calosi, Claudio & Morganti, Matteo (2020) 'Interpreting Quantum Entanglement: Steps towards Coherentist Quantum Mechanics', *British Journal for the Philosophy of Science* 72 (3): 865–91. http://doi:10.1093/bjps/axy064.

Campbell, Keith (1990) *Abstract Particulars.* Oxford: Blackwell.

Correia, Fabrice (2005) *Existential Dependence and Cognate Notions.* Munich: Philosophia.

Correia, Fabrice (2008) 'Ontological Dependence', *Philosophy Compass* 3 (5): 1013–32. http://doi:10.1111/j.1747-9991.2008.00170.x.

Correia, Fabrice (2017) 'Real Definitions', *Philosophical Issues* 27 (1): 52–73. http://doi:10.1111/phis.12091.

Crane, Tim (2003) 'Mental Substances', *Royal Institute of Philosophy Supplement* 53: 229–50.

Dainton, Barry (2008) *The Phenomenal Self.* Oxford: Oxford University Press.

Dasgupta, Shamik (2017) 'Constitutive Explanation', *Philosophical Issues* 27 (1): 74–97. http://doi:10.1111/phis.12102.

Denby, David (2007) 'A Note on Analysing Substancehood', *Australasian Journal of Philosophy* 85 (3): 473–84. http://doi:10.1080/00048400701572238.

deRosset, Louis (2020) 'Anti-Skeptical Rejoinders', in Michael J. Raven (ed.), *The Routledge Handbook of Metaphysical Grounding.* New York: Routledge, 180–93.

Descartes, René (1985 [1644]) 'Principles of Philosophy', in *The Philosophical Writings of Descartes, vol. I* (trans. John Cottingham, Robert Stoothoff & Dugald Murdoch). Cambridge: Cambridge University Press.

Dixon, T. Scott (2016) 'What Is the Well-Foundedness of Grounding?', *Mind* 125 (498): 439–68. http://doi:10.1093/mind/fzv112.

Dorato, Mauro & Morganti, Matteo (2013) 'Grades of Individuality: A Pluralistic View of Identity in Quantum Mechanics and in the Sciences', *Philosophical Studies* 163 (3): 591–610. http://doi 0.1007/s11098-011-9833-z.

Dowell, Janice L. (2006) 'Formulating the Thesis of Physicalism: An Introduction', *Philosophical Studies* 131 (1): 1–23. http://doi:10.1007/s11098-006-6641-y.

Esfeld, Michael (2021) 'Thing and Non-thing Ontologies', in Ricki Bliss & James T. M. Miller (eds.), *The Routledge Handbook of Metametaphysics.* Abingdon: Routledge, 459–67.

Fine, Kit (1995) 'Ontological Dependence', *Proceedings of the Aristotelian Society (New Series)* 95 (1): 269–90.

Fine, Kit (2003) 'The Non-Identity of a Material Thing and Its Matter', *Mind* 112 (446): 195–234.

Foster, John (1991) *The Immaterial Self: A Defence of the Cartesian Dualist Conception of the Mind*. London: Routledge.

French, Steven (2019) 'Identity and Individuality in Quantum Theory', in Edward N. Zalta (ed.), *The Stanford Encyclopedia of Philosophy*. https://plato.stanford.edu/archives/win2019/entries/qt-idind.

Gorman, Michael (2006) 'Substance and Identity-Dependence', *Philosophical Papers* 35 (1): 103–18. http://doi:10.1080/05568640609485174.

Gorman, Michael (2012) 'On Substantial Independence: A Reply to Patrick Toner', *Philosophical Studies* 159 (2): 293–7. http://doi:10.1007/sl 1098-011-9708-3.

Healey, Richard (1995) 'Substance, Modality and Spacetime', *Erkenntnis* 42 (3): 287–316.

Heil, John (2003) *From an Ontological Point of View*. Oxford: Oxford University Press.

Heil, John (2012) *The Universe as We Find It*. Oxford: Oxford University Press.

Hoffman, Joshua (2011) 'Metametaphysics and Substance: Two Case Studies', *Axiomathes* 21 (4): 491–505. http://doi:10.1007/s10516-010-9123-y.

Hoffman, Joshua & Rosenkrantz, Gary S. (1994) *Substance among Other Categories*. Cambridge: Cambridge University Press.

Hoffman, Joshua & Rosenkrantz, Gary S. (1997) *Substance: Its Nature and Existence*. London: Routledge.

Hoffman, Joshua & Rosenkrantz, Gary S. (2007) 'How to Analyse Substance: A Reply to Schnieder', *Ratio* 20 (1): 130–41.

Inman, Ross D. (2018) *Substance and the Fundamentality of the Familiar: A Neo-Aristotelian Mereology*. New York: Routledge.

Ismael, Jenann & Schaffer, Jonathan (2019) 'Quantum Holism: Nonseparability as Common Ground', *Synthese* 197 (10): 4131–60. http://doi:10.1007/s11229-016-1201-2.

Jaworski, William (2016) *Structure and the Metaphysics of Mind: How Hylomorphism Solves the Mind-Body Problem*. Oxford: Oxford University Press.

Jenkins, Carrie S. (2010) 'What is Ontological Realism?', *Philosophy Compass* 5 (10): 880–90. http://doi:10.1111/j.1747-9991.2010.00332.x.

Kim, Jaegwon (1998) *Mind in a Physical World: An Essay on the Mind-Body Problem and Mental Causation*. Cambridge, MA: MIT Press.

Koslicki, Kathrin (2008) *The Structure of Objects*. Oxford: Oxford University Press.

Koslicki, Kathrin (2012) 'Varieties of Ontological Dependence', in Fabrice Correia and Benjamin Schnieder (eds.), *Metaphysical Grounding: Understanding the Structure of Reality*. Cambridge: Cambridge University Press, 186–213.

Koslicki, Kathrin (2015) 'The Coarse-Grainedness of Grounding', *Oxford Studies in Metaphysics* 9: 306–44.

Koslicki, Kathrin (2018) *Form, Matter, Substance*. Oxford: Oxford University Press.

Koslicki, Kathrin (2020) 'Skeptical Doubts', in Michael J. Raven (ed.), *The Routledge Handbook of Metaphysical Grounding*. New York: Routledge, 164–79.

Kronen, John & Tuttle, Jacob (2011) 'Composite Substances as True Wholes: Toward a Nyāya-Vaiśeṣika Theory of Composite Substances', *Canadian Journal of Philosophy* 41 (2): 289–316.

Ladyman, James & Ross, Don, with Spurrett, David & Collier, John (2007) *Every Thing Must Go: Metaphysics Naturalized*. Oxford: Oxford University Press.

Levine, Joseph & Trogdon, Kelly (2009) 'The Modal Status of Materialism', *Philosophical Studies* 145 (3): 351–62, http://doi:10.1007/s11098-008-9235-z.

Lewis, David K. (1983) 'New Work for a Theory of Universals', *Australasian Journal of Philosophy* 61 (4): 343–77.

Loose, Jonathan J., Menuge, Angus J. L. & Moreland, James P. (eds.) (2018) *The Blackwell Companion to Substance Dualism*. Hoboken: Wiley Blackwell.

Loux, Michael J. (1978) *Substance and Attribute: A Study in Ontology*. Dordrecht: D. Reidel.

Loux, Michael J. (2006) *Metaphysics: A Contemporary Introduction* (3rd ed.). New York: Routledge.

Lovejoy, Arthur O. (1964 [1936]) *The Great Chain of Being*. Cambridge, MA: Harvard University Press.

Lowe, E. J. (1996) *Subjects of Experience*. Cambridge: Cambridge University Press.

Lowe, E. J. (1998) *The Possibility of Metaphysics: Substance, Identity, and Time*. Oxford: Oxford University Press.

Lowe, E. J. (2006) *The Four-Category Ontology: A Metaphysical Foundation for Natural Science*. Oxford: Oxford University Press.

Lowe, E. J. (2012) 'Against Monism', in Philip Goff (ed.), *Spinoza on Monism*. Basingstoke: Palgrave, 92–112.

Lowe, E. J. (2013) 'Varieties of Metaphysical Dependence', in Miguel Hoeltje, Benjamin Schnieder & Alex Steinberg (eds.), *Varieties of Dependence: Ontological Dependence, Grounding, Supervenience, Response-Dependence*. Munich: Philosophia, 193–210.

Lowe, E. J. (2016) 'Non-Individuals', in Alexandre Guay & Thomas Pradeu (eds.), *Individuals Across the Sciences*. Oxford: Oxford University Press, 49–60.

Mackie, Penelope (2000) 'Review of *Substance among Other Categories* by J. Hoffman & G. S. Rosenkrantz', *Mind* 109 (433): 149–52.

Mackie, Penelope (2021) 'Persistence and Modality', *Synthese* 198 (6): 1425–38. https://doi.org/10.1007/s11229-018-1776-x.

Madden, Rory (2015) 'The Place of the Self in Contemporary Metaphysics', *Royal Institute of Philosophy Supplement* 76: 77–95. http://doi:10.1017/S1358246115000089.

Mallozzi, Antonella, Vaidya, Anand & Wallner, Michael (2021) 'The Epistemology of Modality', in Edward N. Zalta (ed.), *The Stanford Encyclopedia of Philosophy*. https://plato.stanford.edu/archives/fall2021/entries/modality-epistemology.

Marmodoro, Anna (2021) 'Hylomorphic Unity', in Ricki Bliss & James T. M. Miller (eds.), *The Routledge Handbook of Metametaphysics*. Abingdon: Routledge, 284–99.

Maudlin, Tim (2007) *The Metaphysics Within Physics*. Oxford: Oxford University Press.

McGinn, Marie (2000) 'Real Things and the Mind Body Problem', *Proceedings of the Aristotelian Society (New Series)* 100 (3): 303–17.

McKenzie, Kerry (2021) 'Science-Guided Metaphysics', in Ricki Bliss & James T. M. Miller (eds.), *The Routledge Handbook of Metametaphysics*. Abingdon: Routledge, 435–46.

Melnyk, Andrew (2008) 'Can Physicalism Be Non-Reductive?', *Philosophy Compass* 3 (6): 1281–96. http://doi:10.1111/j.1747-9991.2008.00184.x.

Metzinger, Thomas (2003) *Being No One: The Self-Model Theory of Subjectivity*. Cambridge, MA: MIT Press.

Morgan, William (in press) 'Are Organisms Substances or Processes?', *Australasian Journal of Philosophy*. http://doi:10.1080/00048402.2021.1931378.

Morganti, Matteo (2009) 'Ontological Priority, Fundamentality and Monism', *Dialectica* 63 (3): 271–88. http://doi:10.1111/j.1746-8361.2009.01197.x.

Morganti, Matteo (2018) 'The Structure of Physical Reality: Beyond Foundationalism', in Ricki Bliss & Graham Priest (eds.), *Reality and Its Structure: Essays in Fundamentality*. Oxford: Oxford University Press, 254–72.

Morganti, Matteo (2020) 'Fundamentality in Metaphysics and the Philosophy of Physics. Part II: The Philosophy of Physics', *Philosophy Compass* 15 (10): 1–14. http://doi 10.1111/phc3.12703.

Morganti, Matteo & Tahko, Tuomas E. (2017) 'Moderately Naturalistic Metaphysics', *Synthese* 194 (7): 2557–80. http://doi 10.1007/s11229-016-1068-2.

Mulligan, Kevin, Simons, Peter & Smith, Barry (1984) 'Truth-Makers', *Philosophy and Phenomenological Research* 44 (3): 287–321.

Nolan, Daniel (2011) 'Categories and Ontological Dependence', *Monist* 94 (2): 277–301.

Novotný, Daniel D. & Novák, Lukáš (eds.) (2014) *Neo-Aristotelian Perspectives in Metaphysics*. New York: Routledge.

O'Connor, Timothy & Jacobs, Jonathan D. (2003) 'Emergent Individuals', *Philosophical Quarterly* 53 (213): 540–55.

Oderberg, David S. (2007) *Real Essentialism*. New York: Routledge.

O'Leary-Hawthorne, John & Cover, Jan A. (1998) 'A World of Universals', *Philosophical Studies* 91 (3): 205–19.

Oliver, Alex (1996) 'The Metaphysics of Properties', *Mind* 105 (417): 1–80.

Olson, Eric T. (2007) *What Are We? A Study in Personal Ontology*. Oxford: Oxford University Press.

Pasnau, Robert (2011) *Metaphysical Themes 1274–1671*. Oxford: Oxford University Press.

Raven, Michael J. (2016) 'Fundamentality without Foundations', *Philosophy and Phenomenological Research* 93 (3): 607–26. http://doi:10.1111/phpr.12200.

Raven, Michael J. (2017) 'New Work for a Theory of Ground', *Inquiry* 60 (6): 625–55. http://doi:10.1080/0020174X.2016.1251333.

Raven, Michael J., ed. (2020) *The Routledge Handbook of Metaphysical Grounding*. New York: Routledge.

Rea, Michael (2011) 'Hylomorphism Reconditioned', *Philosophical Perspectives* 25: 341–58. http://doi:10.1111/j.1520-8583.2011.00219.x.

Richardson, Kevin (2020) 'Varieties', in Michael J. Raven (ed.), *The Routledge Handbook of Metaphysical Grounding*. New York: Routledge, 194–208.

Robb, David (2009) 'Substance', in Robin Le Poidevin, Peter Simons, Andrew McGonigal & Ross P. Cameron (eds.), *The Routledge Companion to Metaphysics*. Abingdon: Routledge, pp. 256–64.

Robinson, Howard (2016) *From the Knowledge Argument to Mental Substance: Resurrecting the Mind*. Cambridge: Cambridge University Press.

Robinson, Howard (2021) 'Substance', in Edward N. Zalta (ed.), *The Stanford Encyclopedia of Philosophy*. https://plato.stanford.edu/archives/fall2021/entries/substance/.

Robinson, Tad (n.d.) '17th Century Theories of Substance', in James Fieser & Bradley Dowden (eds.), *Internet Encyclopedia of Philosophy*. https://iep .utm.edu/substanc/.

Russell, Bertrand (1945) *History of Western Philosophy*. London: George Allen and Unwin.

Rydéhn, Henrik (2021) 'Grounding and Ontological Dependence', *Synthese* 198 (6): 1231–56. https://doi.org/10.1007/s11229-018-1818-4.

Schaffer, Jonathan (2003) 'Is There a Fundamental Level?', *Noûs* 37 (3): 498–517.

Schaffer, Jonathan (2004) 'Two Conceptions of Sparse Properties', *Pacific Philosophical Quarterly* 85 (1): 92–102. http://doi:10.1111/j.1468-0114.2004 .00189.x.

Schaffer, Jonathan (2009a) 'On What Grounds What', in David Chalmers, David Manley & Ryan Wasserman (eds.), *Metametaphysics: New Essays on the Foundations of Ontology*. Oxford: Oxford University Press, 347–83.

Schaffer, Jonathan (2009b) 'Spacetime the One Substance', *Philosophical Studies* 145 (1): 131–48. http://doi:10.1007/s11098-009-9386-6.

Schaffer, Jonathan (2010a) 'Monism: The Priority of the Whole', *Philosophical Review* 119 (1): 31–76. http://doi:10.1215/00318108-2009-025.

Schaffer, Jonathan (2010b) 'The Internal Relatedness of All Things', *Mind* 119 (474): 341–76. http://doi:10.1093/mind/fzq033.

Schaffer, Jonathan (2013) 'The Action of the Whole', *Aristotelian Society Supplementary Volume* 87 (1): 67–87. http://doi:10.1111/j.1467-8349 .2013.00220.x.

Schaffer, Jonathan (2018) 'Monism', in Edward N. Zalta (ed.), *The Stanford Encyclopedia of Philosophy*. https://plato.stanford.edu/archives/win2018/ entries/monism.

Schneider, Susan (2012) 'Why Property Dualists Must Reject Substance Physicalism', *Philosophical Studies* 157 (1): 61–76. http://doi:10.1007/s11098-010-9618-9.

Schnieder, Benjamin (2005) 'How Not to Define Substance: A Comment Upon Hoffman and Rosenkrantz', *Ratio* 18 (1): 107–17. http://doi:10.1111/j.1467-9329 .2005.00275.x.

Schnieder, Benjamin (2006) 'A Certain Kind of Trinity: Dependence, Substance, Explanation', *Philosophical Studies* 129 (2): 393–419. http:// doi:10.1007/si1098-005-4636.

Schnieder, Benjamin (2020) 'Grounding and Dependence', *Synthese* 197 (1): 95–124. http://doi:10.1007/s11229-017-1378-z.

Seibt, Johanna (2009) 'Forms of Emergent Interaction in General Process Theory', *Synthese* 166 (3): 479–512. http://doi:10.1007/S11229-008-9373-Z.

Shoemaker, Sydney (1997) 'Self and Substance', *Philosophical Perspectives* 11: 283–304. http://doi:10.1111/0029-4624.31.s11.13.

Sider, Ted (2006) 'Bare Particulars', *Philosophical Perspectives* 20: 287–97. http://doi:10.1111/j.1520-8583.2006.00112.x.

Simons, Peter (1998) 'Farewell to Substance: A Differentiated Leave-Taking', *Ratio* 11 (3): 235–52. http://doi:10.1111/1467-9329.00069.

Snowdon, Paul F. (2014) *Persons, Animals, Ourselves*. Oxford: Oxford University Press.

Spackman, John (2013) 'Consciousness and the Prospects for Substance Dualism', *Philosophy Compass* 8 (11): 1054–65. http://doi:10.1111/phc3.12009.

Steward, Helen (2012) 'Actions as Processes', *Philosophical Perspectives* 26: 373–88. https://doi.org/10.1111/phpe.12008.

Steward, Helen (2020) 'Substances, Agents and Processes', *Philosophy* 95 (1): 41–61. http://doi.org/10.1017/S0031819119000494.

Studtmann, Paul (2021) 'Aristotle's Categories', in Edward N. Zalta (ed.), *The Stanford Encyclopedia of Philosophy*, https://plato.stanford.edu/archives/spr2021/entries/aristotle-categories/.

Swinburne, Richard (2013) *Mind, Brain, and Free Will*. Oxford: Oxford University Press.

Tahko, Tuomas E., ed. (2012) *Contemporary Aristotelian Metaphysics*. Cambridge: Cambridge University Press.

Tahko, Tuomas E. & Lowe, E. J. (2020) 'Ontological Dependence', in Edward N. Zalta (ed.), *The Stanford Encyclopedia of Philosophy*. https://plato.stanford.edu/archives/fall2020/entries/dependence-ontological.

Tallant, Jonathan (2015) 'Ontological Dependence in a Space-time World', *Philosophical Studies* 172 (11): 3101–18. http://doi:10.1007/s11098-015-0459-4.

Thompson, Naomi (2018a) 'Irrealism about Grounding', *Royal Institute of Philosophy Supplement* 82: 23–44. http://doi:10.1017/S1358246118000206.

Thompson, Naomi (2018b) 'Metaphysical Interdependence, Epistemic Coherentism, and Holistic Explanation', in Ricki Bliss & Graham Priest (eds.), *Reality and Its Structure: Essays in Fundamentality*. Oxford: Oxford University Press, 107–25.

Thompson, Naomi (2020) 'Strict Partial Order', in Michael J. Raven (ed.), *The Routledge Handbook of Metaphysical Grounding*. New York: Routledge, 259–70.

Toner, Patrick (2008) 'Emergent Substance', *Philosophical Studies* 141 (3): 281–97. http://doi:10.1007/s11098-007-9160-6.

Toner, Patrick (2011) 'Independence Accounts of Substance and Substantial Parts', *Philosophical Studies* 155 (1): 37–43. http://doi:10.1007/sl 1098-010-9521-4.

Trogdon, Kelly (2018) 'Grounding-Mechanical Explanation', *Philosophical Studies* 175 (6): 1289–309. https://doi.org/10.1007/s11098-017-0911-8.

Van Cleve, James (1985) 'Three Versions of the Bundle Theory', *Philosophical Studies* 47 (1): 95–107.

Van Cleve, James (1990) 'Mind-Dust or Magic? Panpsychism versus Emergence', *Philosophical Perspectives* 4: 215–26.

Van Inwagen, Peter (1990) *Material Beings*. Ithaca: Cornell University Press.

Van Inwagen, Peter (1993) *Metaphysics*. Boulder: Westview Press.

Wang, Jennifer (2016) 'Fundamentality and Modal Freedom', *Philosophical Perspectives* 30: 397–418. http://doi:10.1111/phpe.12082.

Wang, Jennifer (2019) 'The Essences of Fundamental Properties', *Metaphysics* 2 (1): 40–54. http://doi:10.5334/met.29.

Weir, Ralph Stefan (2021) 'Bring Back Substances!', *Review of Metaphysics* 75 (2): 265–308.

Westerhoff, Jan (2005) *Ontological Categories: Their Nature and Significance*. Oxford: Oxford University Press. http://doi:10.1093/acprof:oso/9780199285044.001.0001.

Wiggins, David (1980) *Sameness and Substance*. Oxford: Blackwell.

Wiggins, David (2016) *Continuants: Their Activity, Their Being and Their Identity (Twelve Essays)*. Oxford: Oxford University Press.

Williamson, Timothy (1994) *Vagueness*. Abingdon: Routledge.

Wilson, Jessica M. (2014) 'No Work for a Theory of Grounding', *Inquiry* 57 (5–6): 535–79.

Woolhouse, Roger (1993) *Descartes, Spinoza, and Leibniz: The Concept of Substance in Seventeenth-Century Metaphysics*. New York: Routledge.

Wüthrich, Christian (2019) 'The Emergence of Space and Time', in Sophie Gibb, Robin Hendry & Tom Lancaster (eds.), *The Routledge Handbook of Emergence*. Abingdon: Routledge, 315–26.

Yang, Eric (2015) 'The Compatibility of Property Dualism and Substance Materialism', *Philosophical Studies* 172 (12): 3211–19. http://doi:10.1007/s11098-015-0465-6.

Acknowledgements

Thanks to Claudio Calosi, Elisa Bezençon, Kathrin Koslicki, Olley Pearson, Ralph Weir, Tuomas Tahko, Victor Dura-Villa, and two anonymous referees for their comments on various parts of the manuscript. Thanks also to Tuomas for his invaluable editorial assistance. My work on this Element was supported by the Swiss National Science Foundation (decision number 100012_189031/1). Lastly, I would like to express my gratitude to the late E. J. Lowe, who fostered my interest in metaphysics in general and substance ontology in particular.

Cambridge Elements ☰

Metaphysics

Tuomas E. Tahko
University of Bristol

Tuomas E. Tahko is Professor of Metaphysics of Science at the University of Bristol. Tahko specializes in contemporary analytic metaphysics, with an emphasis on methodological and epistemic issues: 'meta-metaphysics'. He also works at the interface of metaphysics and philosophy of science: 'metaphysics of science'. Tahko is the author of *Unity of Science* (Cambridge University Press, 2021, Elements in Philosophy of Science), *An Introduction to Metametaphysics* (Cambridge University Press, 2015) and editor of *Contemporary Aristotelian Metaphysics* (Cambridge University Press, 2012).

About the Series
This highly accessible series of Elements provides brief but comprehensive introductions to the most central topics in metaphysics. Many of the Elements also go into considerable depth, so the series will appeal to both students and academics. Some Elements bridge the gaps between metaphysics, philosophy of science, and epistemology.

Cambridge Elements ≡

Metaphysics

Elements in the Series

A full series listing is available at: www.cambridge.org/EMPH

Printed in the United States
by Baker & Taylor Publisher Services